# CLIVE

MILITARY PROFILES
Series Editor
*Dennis E. Showalter, Ph.D.*
*Colorado College*

*Instructive summaries for general and expert*
*readers alike, volumes in the Military Profiles*
*series are essential treatments of significant and*
*popular military figures drawn from world history,*
*ancient times through the present.*

# CLIVE

Founder of British India

*C. Brad Faught*

**Potomac Books**
*Washington, D.C.*

**Library of Congress Cataloging-in-Publication Data**
Faught, C. Brad.
   Clive : founder of British India / C. Brad Faught. — First Edition.
     pages cm. — (Military profiles)
   Includes bibliographical references and index.
   ISBN 978-1-61234-168-2 (hardcover : alk. paper)
   ISBN 978-1-61234-169-9 (electronic)
   1. Clive, Robert Clive, Baron, 1725–1774. 2. India—History—British occupation, 1765–1947—Biography. 3. India—History—18th century. 4. East India Company—History—18th century. 5. Generals—Great Britain—Biography. 6. Generals—India—Biography. 7. Governors—India—Biography. I. Title.
   DS471.F38 2013
   954.02'9092—dc23
   [B]

                         2012040605

Potomac Books
22841 Quicksilver Drive
Dulles, Virginia 20166

First Edition

10 9 8 7 6 5 4 3 2 1

To the memory of a beloved uncle,
Hugh Blagdon Tunnicliffe (1919–2010)

# *Contents*

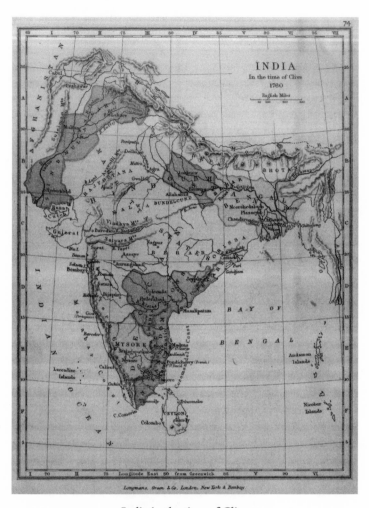

**India in the time of Clive**

The Indian subcontinent c. 1760. *Courtesy of the University of Texas Libraries, The University of Texas at Austin*

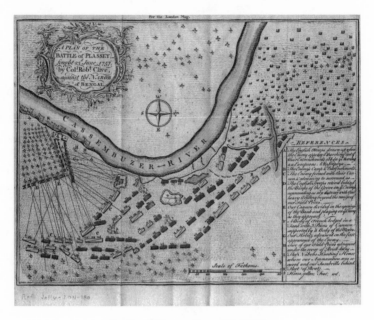

**Battle of Plassey, June 23, 1757**
The disposition of forces. *Author's collection*

# *Preface*

"By God, at this moment, do I stand astonished at my own moderation!" So said Robert Lord Clive in 1772 in stout defense of his embattled record and impugned reputation to the House of Commons Select
Committee on Indian Affairs. He was referring, of course, to the enormous plunder that was at his disposal after defeating the Nawab of
Bengal in June 1757 at Plassey, a military victory that propelled might-
ily the fortunes of both the East India Company and Clive himself,
foreshadowing the dawn of British India. Clive, naturally, was amply
rewarded for the victory but certainly never believed what others came
to later understand was a scarcely hidden avariciousness that enabled
a cadre of company servants—with Clive seen to be at their head—to
come home from India as rich as the "oriental despots" they had
unseated. Clive's historical reputation has always labored under a pall
of assumptions about ill-gotten gain, but in the annals of British
Imperial history such now is almost moot. That is to say, Clive's
supremely important position in the establishment of British (company) rule in Bengal proved to be the egg from which Britain's Indian
empire was hatched, and whether his acquired riches were greater than
they were entitled to be is not a question that need trouble modern
biographers of the man at length.

   This examination of Clive—the first in almost a generation and
one of the few that concentrates on him mainly as a military leader—
seeks to place Clive squarely in the run of the times in which he lived.
In recent years, India has enjoyed a remarkable rise in world economic
affairs, the like of which—one may consider for the sake of historical
argument—might be akin to the way in which Clive and his fellow company men would have viewed the sterling economic prospects of India

in their own time. Inherent in Clive's own economic aspirations, however, was a necessary military element, especially in the form of Britain's chief European rival, France, as well as internal Indian competitors who fell under the increasingly shaky suzerainty of the two-hundred-year-old Mughal Empire. Altogether, success in the burgeoning India trade depended on gaining monopolies over commerce in indigo, jute, tea, and a number of other products for which the market in Britain and elsewhere in Europe was rapidly growing. The participants in the India trade were mercantilists to a man, and therefore they understood trade to be an all-or-nothing enterprise in which a rival's success necessarily imperiled one's own. Accordingly, successful trade was that which wrested it away from your opponent's control, which meant, ultimately, reliance on the strength of the sword. Brandishing the sword in the name of the East India Company was what Robert Clive became exceedingly good at within a few years of his arrival at Madras in 1744, and it set him up for a career's worth of power, wealth, and social advancement.

Even though this biography endeavors to tell Clive's life story through the lens of military history, as in all good histories of this type there is more to it than mere marching. Clive was a headstrong and ambitious man, perhaps even vulgar, and no telling of his life can be considered complete without recognizing that alongside the contemporary military and commercial achievements were features of his character that are not the least bit attractive—not then, and not now. Fortunately, at this late remove from the age in which he lived, Clive's life can be examined without the need to either justify or excoriate, but rather simply to try to understand his motivations and actions. As Clive is an arresting figure of great significance in the history of the British Empire in India, there is no shortage of biographies of him (see bibliographical note); this one, however, unlike many of those that have come before, intends neither to "take sides" nor to act as an apologia, but rather to offer an unvarnished assessment of Clive's life and work as a military commander in the service of a commercial enterprise: a captain of industry, indeed.

The writing of books is a collaborative exercise, and I am happy to acknowledge the many people who have helped me research and write this one. I offer my sincere thanks to Elizabeth Demers, senior editor at Potomac Books, for bringing this study of Clive to fruition, as well as to the other Potomac staff members. This book is my second one with Potomac, and both experiences have been thoroughly enjoyable.

Thanks, also, to the staff of the British Library in London and the National Library of Wales in Aberystwyth. Working in these superb institutions, assisted by their expert archivists and librarians, was a constant pleasure. My visit to Powis Castle and its Clive Museum in Wales was highly enjoyable and rewarding, and I thank their staff for making it so. Equally rewarding was a journey to Moreton Say in Shropshire, Clive's home village and the place where he is buried in the parish church, along with nearby Styche Hall, the former Clive family seat. A visit to Walcot Hall in south Shropshire, Clive's main country home that he acquired in 1763, was made possible by the current owner, Robin Parish, through building supervisor Maria Higgs, to whom I am grateful. I would also like to express my thanks to Tyndale University College in Toronto, where I teach, for granting me a sabbatical during which time this book was researched and written. The Travellers Club in London, where I enjoy membership, and Massey College at the University of Toronto, where I am a senior fellow—were equally wonderful "homes away from home" during the time I spent working on this book. I thank them both for their hospitality and for environments highly conducive to book writing. I would like to thank my wife, Rhonda, and our children, Claire and Luke, without whom this book could not have been written and whose love and support are worth more than words can say.

Lastly, I have dedicated this book to my late uncle, Hugh Blagdon (Bud) Tunnicliffe. Sadly, he died before I had begun work on it, but it is just the sort of book that he would have greatly enjoyed reading. In days gone by he was very generous in assisting me to study in England, and dedicating this book to him is a small token of my appreciation for that, as well as for much else besides.

# *Chronology*

# A Shropshire Lad

IN THE EARLY EIGHTEENTH CENTURY the county of Shropshire was an out-of-the-way part of England. In our own day it is considered by some to be part of the so-called Heart of England, but then such was not the case. Highly appealing nonetheless, the pleasant Shropshire countryside rolls westward right up to the Welsh border. Its topography is a mixture of flatlands and serrated hills, but a deep green predominates everywhere, broken then—before the mid-nineteenth-century advent of the railway—only by rutted roads, narrow lanes, and small villages, the majority of which date from the medieval era. Included among them was Moreton Say, a tiny village then as now, located a few miles outside the town of Market Drayton and a few more still from the county town of Shrewsbury. An unprepossessing burgh, Shrewsbury was nonetheless at the center of Shropshire's economic and commercial life, the place that Salopians—as the county's residents are called—saw as vital to their communal prosperity. And around nearby Moreton Say few Salopians were more prosperous or important than the Clives.

The Clive family had been in the area for hundreds of years. They dated themselves there as far back as the twelfth century, taking their name from the local village of Clive. Since then they had raised themselves to the level of county gentry—if not of the grandest type. Like other such families they sought royal favor and gratefully achieved it in the person of Sir George Clive, a prominent government official at the sixteenth-century Tudor court. In the next century, the Clive name was carried into the midst of the English Civil War by Col. Robert Clive, a fierce partisan of Cromwell's parliamentary cause.[1] Altogether by the eighteenth century, the Clives—centered on their rather modest but firmly planted family seat of Styche Hall—were the leading family of their corner of Shropshire.

Richard Clive, our Robert Clive's father, was the proud occupant of Styche Hall, then still a simple half-timbered structure before it was considerably enlarged with some of the wealth later gained in India. Born around 1694, Richard Clive had been educated locally and then went on to qualify as a barrister. He also, in later years, would be elected as a member of Parliament (MP) for the nearby constituency of Montgomeryshire. Throughout he had worked hard to build a metropolitan law practice in London, but without great success, so it was the income generated by the Styche estate—some £500 annually (the modern equivalent of about US$150,000)—that kept the family name respectable and their station in society moderately high. An income of this amount meant that the Clives were solid members of the English upper-middle class, a status that captured about 40,000 families at that time in the country's history, perhaps 10 percent of the total.[2] Confirming Richard Clive's gentility was his marriage to Rebecca Gaskell. Born about 1700, she came from a respectable Manchester family, and one of her descendants would later marry the woman who became the famous Victorian novelist, Elizabeth Gaskell.

Robert Clive, the couple's first child, was born at Styche Hall on September 29, 1725. He would be the first of thirteen children—an inadvertent nod to later Malthusian assumptions about population growth—but of this large number only seven of them (five girls and two boys) survived infancy.[3] Unlike those unfortunates among his younger siblings, however, Clive was a strong and healthy child, and critically, he was not felled by any of the usual maladies—diphtheria, whooping cough, measles, and others—that regularly carried off children of the time. His first three years were spent at Styche Hall, but in 1728 the young Clive was sent away to live with his aunt (his mother's sister) and uncle, Elizabeth and Daniel Bayley, in their comfortable home, Hope Hall, just outside Manchester. There he would remain for the next six years, until his beloved "Aunt May," as Elizabeth was called, died. It is unclear why Clive's parents chose to send him off at such a tender age, but doing so was certainly not an unusual move for a family of means in the 1720s. Indeed, such a practice would only deepen in the eighteenth century, and further still in the nineteenth, when sending boys away from home—especially to board at public schools—became a cultural touchstone in Britain. But likely much more pressing for the Clives in 1728 was Rebecca's rapid succession of pregnancies, the result of which had been the birth and death of three sons in the years immediately following Robert's birth.[4]

Upon his aunt's death in 1734, Clive's six happy years at Hope Hall came to an end. He returned home to Styche, to a house that was almost unknown to him; its occupants were equally strange as they now included a surviving younger brother and four sisters. Meanwhile, Clive's education continued apace. From a school at Bostock, Cheshire, he transferred to the Old Grammar School located next to the parish church of St. Mary's in nearby Drayton, as the town of Market Drayton was then called. From there, in 1737, he moved on to the best school he would ever attend, Merchant Taylors' in London, and then, finally, to a kind of vocational establishment in Hemel Hempstead run by a certain Mr. Sterling, where Clive learned the intricacies of working with figures and of double-entry bookkeeping—skills that would later come to be of great value to him in India.

In none of these schools, however, did the youthful Clive distinguish himself: he was certainly no academic high-flyer. But neither was he unintelligent. Clive had always been fiery and physical. His uncle Daniel had spoken of trying to suppress the "hero" in him.[5] He had grown quite tall for his time—eventually to about six feet—and strong, sure of himself among his peers, and confident socially because of his relatively prominent family status, at least locally. His peripatetic education perhaps matched a similarly roving childhood. In any event, by the time Clive reached seventeen years of age in the autumn of 1742 he was close enough to manhood for his father to think hard about the vocation or profession for which he might be best-suited. Ultimately he settled on seeking a place for him in the leading merchant trading house of the day, the East India Company, the headquarters of which were located square in the middle of the City of London on Leadenhall Street.

The East India Company, or the Governor and Company of Merchants of London Trading into the East Indies as it was known officially at its founding on December 31, 1600, had come into existence during the waning days of Elizabeth I's long reign. In the years before it succeeded in being granted a trading charter, a group of London merchants had sought permission from the Crown to sail to the Indian Ocean in an exploratory attempt to place the English amid the lucrative European overseas trade in prized spices such as pepper and nutmeg. Such permission was eventually granted, and in 1591 three ships had left England. Only one returned, however, the *Edward Bonaventure*, but critically it did so with a cargo of spices and tales of great riches to be had around the Malay Peninsula in the South Pacific. On the strength of that first voyage more ships followed in 1596, although all of them were lost at sea. Nevertheless, the London merchants were determined to keep trying, and two years later—and on the basis of some £30,000 in raised capital—they met to form a corporation. The Queen, advised by her ministers that granting a charter to the London men would provoke the competing Spanish, declined to do so. But the spice trade lobbyists remained persistent in their cause. The next year they met again, having raised yet more capital and having purchased new ships as evidence of their commitment to the enterprise. The Queen, impressed by their doggedness and convinced of the merits of their economic case, finally granted them a Royal Charter on the final day of the seventeenth century. This charter awarded the Earl of Cumberland, their leader, and his fellow 215 investors in the East India Company, a monopoly of English trade with all countries east of the Cape of Good Hope and west of the Straits of Magellan. And in 1601, the chartered company sent off on its maiden voyage under the command of Sir James Lancaster.

The East India Company's earliest years were challenging and unsuccessful, however, as it sought to gain a foothold in the highly rewarding spice trade. In this last century before the acknowledged advent of Adam Smith's capitalist economics, the major European states remained firm practitioners of mercantilism. That is to say, trade was believed to be a mutually exclusive enterprise, with one country's enrichment only possible at the expense of another's. Spain, Portugal, and the Netherlands all had a leg up on England in this regard, and so for the infant company its initial foray into the field was essentially one of trying to catch up to its better-positioned rivals. Occasionally this meant the outbreak of fighting, such as that against England's main early rival, the Portuguese, in 1612 at the Battle of Swally. But by that time the English had already established their first foothold, at Surat, located on the west coast of India, in 1611. Success here prompted the company to consider the possibility of making its presence a permanent one in India, a move that could only be made with the blessing of the Mughal emperor, Jahangir, whose lavish court was located a thousand miles inland at Agra. The way forward in this regard had been paved a few years earlier by William Hawkins, an intrepid if rumbustious company emissary, who had traveled to the Mughal capital in 1609. Despite initial success in persuading the emperor to offer the English the right to a fortified factory at Surat—a campaign that included Hawkins marrying the daughter of a deceased Armenian Christian trader who had gained favor at the court of the great Akbar, Jahangir's father and illustrious predecessor—his mission was not a success. By the autumn of 1611 Hawkins had duly left Agra, frustrated to distraction that the Portuguese continued to win the day in convincing the Mughals that if the English were the other possible European trading option, then the Portuguese themselves remained still the better partner.

The English company would continue to be thwarted in this way until 1615. In that year the Court of Directors, under whose control the company's business was conducted, dispatched Sir Thomas Roe, a career diplomat and sometime Member of Parliament, to approach the emperor once again. Consequently, Roe would spend the next three years wooing Jahangir: "I am yet following this wandering King over mountaynes and through woods, so strange and unused wayes," he reported home.[6] But this time, the full power of the Crown, of James I (who had succeeded Queen Elizabeth upon her death in 1603), would be behind the bid for a full-blown commercial treaty. In exchange for the right to build a factory at Surat and in other areas of Mughal India, the company would supply the royal court at Agra with all manner of goods from the European market. Delighted at being treated in this august way by a Western power, Jahangir accepted the terms of the proposed treaty: "I have given my general command to all the kingdoms and ports of my dominions to receive all the merchants of the English nation," and the East India Company thus gained its entrée into the Indian subcontinent, its putative position now confirmed. The treaty was indeed, as most accounts agree, "a landmark in the relations between England and India."[7]

In the years that followed, the treaty's provisions unfolded in just the way the Court of Directors had hoped as the East India Company expanded its operations along coastal India. To its bridgehead at Surat were added those at Madras in 1639, Bombay in 1668, and Calcutta in 1690. Indeed, these three locations were major factories, "presidencies" as they were designated by the company. But to them could be added some twenty other smaller factories, which, by the beginning of the eighteenth century, had made the English company powerful, prosperous, and vying with the Dutch and the French (the Portuguese position had by then declined) for regional ascendancy. By this time too, successive British governments were highly enamored of the steadily expanding profits that the company accrued, a significant part of which flowed into the Royal Treasury. From James I's renewal of the company's charter in 1609, to Oliver Cromwell's doing of the same in 1657, to the 1670s when Charles II granted it the right to acquire territory, mint money, engage in war, and exercise civil and criminal jurisdiction over the territories under its command, the company had moved from strength to strength. Indeed, by the early 1700s, it was the most powerful commercial entity in Britain, responsible for fully one-quarter of all imports into the realm. And in India (and ever so tentatively now in China too), as well as elsewhere, the East India Company had become the sharp end of the British imperial stick abroad.

Such was the roiling business enterprise that the young Robert Clive joined when he was appointed to serve at Fort St. George, Madras as a "writer," or clerk, on December 15, 1742.[8] Richard Clive's pastoral responsibility for his son extended fortuitously to having a friend on the company's Court of Directors. From this timely connection had come the younger Clive's consideration for an appointment, which was then confirmed in person by interview. Upon this confirmation Clive was made a minor part of the richest commercial operation in Britain. But his was a desirable appointment nonetheless, even if it had come at the bottom of the ladder. The potential for riches was there, and so too was the opportunity for adventure and romance. One can imagine that at the age of seventeen and with his enterprising temperament, Robert Clive was about as happy as it is possible for a young man to be. A little less than three months later, on March 10, 1743, therefore, he traveled across London to the company's East India Docks located on the Isle of Dogs, said good-bye to his parents who looked on with a mixture of pride and trepidation, and boarded a rather small, mean-looking 500-ton bark, the *Winchester*, then just setting sail for the Far East. And with that, Clive departed for India, which was about six months' sailing and ten thousand miles away.

500 Ton Bark - ? Ship?

# Clive's Passage to India

IN 1743, VOYAGING OUT TO INDIA was a rather precarious venture—as it would remain for a good many years to come. The Suez Canal, which would cut the length of the long passage by at least half, was still more than a century away. Those who bid farewell to their loved ones in Portsmouth, Southampton, or London, as Clive's parents did, were keenly aware that they might easily never see them again. Death came in many and varied ways en route to, or once in, India and elsewhere in the East, and the two million European graves dug there from the sixteenth to the twentieth centuries stand in stark testament to this sad fact.[1] But as an adventurous seventeen-year-old, embarking on a life-changing passage, Clive likely didn't entertain such gloomy thoughts on that March day of departure at the windswept East India Docks.

Down the Thames went the *Winchester* with Clive onboard, the great river's estuary opening up before them. And then with the ship's sails billowing in the wind, it slid out into the English Channel. The Atlantic was raised, Europe fell away, Gibraltar passed by, and then the small ship sidled up to Africa, then wholly unknown by Europeans beyond its slave-supplying coasts. The *Winchester*, despite its relatively small size, was a modern East Indiaman. As befit his station in the company, however, Clive's quarters were cramped and odorous. On board life was governed, as always on these floating wooden worlds, by a social hierarchy that was maintained as strictly at sea as it was on land. For Clive, this meant a very lowly position indeed. He dined and conversed with his fellow juniors, with little but perfunctory contact with either his superiors or with the crew lodged, literally, beneath him. Time passed slowly, and his purse of money (his father had sent him abroad with the not-inconsiderable sum of £54) gradually thinned in the face of the captain's apparent rapacity concerning the cost of the journey's necessities, for which passengers were required to pay. The amount that Clive had left home with was entirely reasonable for a projected six-month passage; yet those six-months ballooned into fifteen on account of the ship's grounding off the coast of Brazil.

The *Winchester* had made for South America in the navigational pattern typical of the time. In order to catch the prevailing easterly trade winds required to propel a ship around the proverbial graveyard that was the Cape of Good Hope, captains routinely sailed their craft diagonally to the Brazilian or Argentine coast, and then back across the Atlantic in a corresponding diagonal to the southern tip of Africa, before heading northward for India. Capt. Gabriel Steward of the *Winchester* had done this route exactly, only to have disaster strike near the Brazilian port of Pernambuco when his ship ran aground. Unable to free the stranded vessel owing to extremely heavy seas, Steward simply anchored it in place, and the officers and crew eventually offloaded to the nearby coast. In the confusion and desperation that accompanied the crisis when it was feared that the ship might sink, Clive lost a number of possessions and was himself later swept overboard only to be saved by the hand of the captain. Being plucked from the raging Atlantic did wonders to alter Clive's hitherto negative opinion of Captain Steward, whom Clive believed, as previously noted, was exorbitant in his ship-board prices and therefore the author of his growing financial woes. In any event, his life saved, Clive settled down to some nine months in Brazil, an unexpected if not unpleasant interregnum in his passage to India.

Brazil in those days was the leading colony in Portugal's seaborne empire. Divided into twelve territorial captaincies that owed their original colonial-era wealth to sugar cultivation and the importation of thousands of African slaves, Pernambuco was in their vanguard. Located at the tip of that part of Brazil, which juts farthest out into the Atlantic Ocean, it had been contested and won by the Dutch in the seventeenth century. Ever since 1500 when Pedro Álvares Cabral had commanded a Portuguese fleet in the landing and colonization of Brazil, Pernambuco had been the most coveted area of the colony. Accordingly, in 1630 the Dutch had successfully attacked and occupied it, remaining in power until 1654 when the resurgent Portuguese pushed them out of what the Dutch had peremptorily declared was their own colony of New Holland. The Portuguese thought otherwise of course, and by the end of the century, gold had replaced sugar as the most important of Brazil's exports with the Portuguese being as starry-eyed over gold as have been all others seduced by the metal's monetarist power.

Upon Clive's arrival in the Portuguese colony some half century later in September 1743, he would have noticed the natural fertility of the land: the Pernambuco coastal forests then were still thick and full. The air was exceptionally humid, and Clive spent his days and nights there writhed in a blanket of damp clothes, "just as if they had been dip't in a river"—a suitable foretaste though of what to expect in India.[2] His almost half year in Pernambuco—the process of towing the *Winchester* into port after four months of bobbing offshore in uncooperative seas, followed by a protracted repair, meant that Clive did not leave until February 1744—were a mixture of ennui, "intollerable heat," cultural exchange, and dissolute living.[3] Young and highly impressionable, Clive explored the port and its environs, socialized on a limited scale, and perhaps sampled the fleshly wares of Pernambuco's prostitutes. Naturally, he had the local language thrust upon him but did not resist learning it—"I have thoroughly instructed myself in the Portugeese language"—a process he would never repeat, however, in any of India's myriad languages.[4] Alas, his money finally did run out, and he needed a loan from Captain Steward to pay for his continued subsistence. The ship's repairs lasted interminably until at last seaworthiness was determined to have been met in February, the anchor was weighed, and the *Winchester* made for the Cape. Smooth sailing ensued, until not far from their destination an exceptionally heavy and damaging gale blew up, necessitating an almost-two-week stopover in

Cape Town for yet more repairs. Settled first by the intrepid Dutchman Jan van Riebeeck in 1652, Cape Town was a neat, orderly, and strategically important outpost, which the British would eventually decide to make their own in 1806 during the Napoleonic Wars. As it was, Clive sat through yet another unscheduled stop before departing finally on the last leg of the journey to India in March 1744.

Almost three months of uneventful and therefore welcome sailing later, on June 1, Clive and his compatriots at last caught sight of India. The southern Coromandel Coast stretched out before them, their destination the port of Madras. Arriving there later that day, the much repaired but still sturdily afloat *Winchester* was anchored in the roads off Fort St. George, the hub of the settlement. Chosen by East India Company agent Francis Day in 1639 as a suitable site for operations in South India, the fort had grown into an important company presidency.[5] Such importance certainly belied its utter uselessness as a natural harbor, however, and no ship approaching Madras welcomed the prospect of negotiating its pounding surf and the necessity thereby of anchoring offshore and dispensing its human and material cargo via a fleet of jetty, or *masula*, boats. Clive's entry into India was by way of just such a modest craft. He had arrived at Madras during the hottest of South India's serial hot seasons, when temperatures soared routinely to more than a 100 degrees Fahrenheit, turning a person's clothes into so much sopping filament. But he had made it nonetheless; almost fifteen months after setting out from London he safely arrived in India. He was eighteen years old, penniless, and thousands of miles from home. Still, he had the comfort of a good position waiting for him and the prospect of the wealth to which it might lead. Clive's great Indian adventure had begun.

More than a hundred years since its founding, Madras had grown into a thriving city of some forty thousand people. At the core of the settlement were about four hundred Europeans, who lodged almost exclusively within the walls of Fort St. George. This traditional star-shaped fortress was complete with bastions, battlements, and church, the latter—the redoubtable St. Mary's—within whose neogothic walls Clive would later marry. Consecrated in 1680, this Church of England sentinel was the first of its kind in the East and stood at the center of the fort, where it stands to this day, the oldest British building in India.

Madras had grown into the East India Company's chief subcontinental settlement, its location putting it squarely within a hotly contested zone in South India, the Carnatic—as the English called the region of Karnataka—which meant a head-to-head struggle with the rival French *Compagnie des Indes*. Just a hundred miles to the south of Madras sat Pondicherry, the main French settlement along the Coromandel coastline. Taken from the Dutch in 1673 as part of Louis XIV's concerted overseas expansion that counted North America's New France as its chief success, occupying Pondicherry was the brainchild of Jean-Baptiste Colbert, the king's brilliant and ambitious finance minister. Their Indian outpost had grown quickly and become an effective base from which the French could penetrate the southern interior, in the same way that Chandernagore, its northern counterpart, was doing in Bengal. Both the English and the French operated locally at the pleasure of the Nawab of the Carnatic, whose position was maintained by his superior, the Nizam of the Deccan, the viceroy, or *subadar*, of the Mughal emperor. The Europeans had won their trading rights on sufferance, all of them continually jockeying to maintain the favor of an easily influenced nawab. Trade was wholly political in nature, and currying Mughal royal favor the ultimate end of intra-European competition.

Clive's arrival at Madras in 1744 had come at a moment of intensifying Anglo-French tension, which would yield more than a decade's worth of intermittent fighting between the old rivals beginning that year, the heart of which would be known as the Seven Years' War (or, as it is called in the United States, the French and Indian War), fought from 1756 until 1763. In 1744, however, that war was still a dozen years and, in the main, a continent away. But its Eastern theater was beginning to take clear shape, with the Madras-Pondicherry corridor its axis.

Clive's first months in Madras, however, were naturally not devoted to understanding the local geostrategic concerns of two great European powers; rather, he was overwhelmingly concerned with learning the ways of the company and finding his feet in a strange country. Initially, Clive lived in the writers' hostel within the fort, his own couple of rooms adequate for the purpose. He was given his lodgings free of charge, on top of which came an allowance for food and other necessities, which included servants (then, as now, manpower being cheap and readily available in India). His salary was a paltry £5 per annum, but it was really more of an honorarium as his real income would come from the privileged trading position held by the company and the accompanying right of its servants to trade on their own account. Indeed, as has been seen, money was an ongoing concern for Clive. In one of the first letters he wrote home after arriving in Madras, he outlined his rather pressing financial position to his father. After writing that he was in a "perfect state of health," Clive noted that he had been obliged to borrow over ten pounds from Captain Steward for "necessaries." This outlay had meant that any "Europe stuffs" that could be sent out—"cloths with their trimmings, also some wigs, shoes, and hats"— would be appreciated. And, in an attempt to ward off the expected censoriousness of Richard Clive, he had also impressed upon him the necessity of wine, "as there are no other sort of drinkables here but that."[6]

In acclimating both to the company and Madras, Clive was hardly alone. He was joined by a number of other young servants, some of whom, like him, were fresh from England. Among this group of company juniors was Edmund (Mun) Maskelyne, who arrived not long after Clive and would prove to be the best friend of his youth, as well as the brother of the woman he would eventually marry, Margaret Maskelyne. Together they learned their jobs, essentially the not-very-interesting one of tallying figures, along with the slightly more engaging one of haggling with Indian suppliers. The temptations and excitements offered by the whirl of life outside the fort represented by the teeming thousands of "Black Town," attracted them during their leisure hours, however. "I can assure you my stay in this place is in every respect pleasant," he wrote home.[7] Youthful pride and bravado are evident in this and other missives to Richard and Rebecca Clive, but Clive experienced wistfulness too, even unhappiness, as is clear in a letter he wrote to his cousin George Clive early in 1745: "I have not enjoyed one happy day since I left my native country."[8]

To someone of Clive's active and physical temperament, bookkeeping was clearly not of sufficient excitement to maintain his prolonged engagement. Meanwhile, the reading of literary books was a pastime that he had begun to cultivate assiduously in the early months and years he spent at Madras. The governor of the settlement from shortly after Clive's arrival, Nicholas Morse, was bookish and accordingly kept a relatively well-stocked library, access to which he offered to company servants. Clive, it seems, exercised the privilege constantly. For someone whose formal education had ended at seventeen he unsurprisingly developed into an autodidact. The library held a large number of religious books and Bibles, as well as a run of the classics.[9] Clive read his way through many of them, the better to be prepared, one supposes, for twice-daily attendance at divine service that was demanded of all company servants. Long hours in the library seemed to also have the effect of calming his rather dyspeptic character and improving the quality of his writing and speech. Clive was a teenager, after all, and despite the hurried-up maturation provided by his appointment and the long voyage out to India, he was still in that wonderfully osmotic time of life when knowledge poured into him as if from a spigot. Increasingly, however, that knowledge was not of the Synoptic Gospels and Aristotle, but rather of the vulnerable position that Fort St. George occupied in the closely contested Carnatic.

The intensification of Anglo-French animosity in the region, occasioned by the faraway War of the Austrian Succession, made itself plain to Clive early on in his stay at Madras. A few years earlier, in 1742, François Dupleix, late the director of the northern French commercial outpost of Chandernagore, had been appointed governor of Pondicherry. He was determined to push French trading and imperial ambitions in South India to their maximum level, and with assistance by Adm. Bernard la Bourdonnais from the French base at the Île de France (today's Mauritius), French regional aspirations soared. Sparring between the two powers thus ensued, reaching an early climax on September 19, 1746, when the French fleet under la Bourdonnais first chased away the overmatched British squadron, and then landed at Fort St. George. A bombardment followed. Two days later, Governor Morse surrendered the outmanned and rapidly undisciplined garrison to la Bourdonnais. Suddenly, the East India Company found that its fortunes in the South had been reduced to the holding of tiny Fort St. David located more than a hundred miles down the coast and, critically, on the other side of Pondicherry.[10]

The taking of Fort St. George was a rather ignominious event for Governor Morse and his men. Luckily for them, la Bourdonnais exercised a good degree of what remained of old medieval-inspired French chivalry. Primarily interested in the fort and its bulging stores, he communicated to Morse terms of lenience: the garrison would be disarmed, its men put on parole (that is, effectively made free), and, for a ransom, the town would be returned to the British. In effect, the bombardment and occupation were turning into a commercial raiding operation, mainly, it became increasingly apparent, for the personal benefit of la Bourdonnais. At Pondicherry, meanwhile, this sequence of events was nonetheless displeasing to Dupleix, who saw the fall of Fort St. George not simply as a commercial windfall but rather as a major first step in the potential pushing out of the region the British company altogether. He therefore made his disapproval immediately known to la Bourdonnais, especially about the ransom demand that he saw correctly as a means by which his subordinate could line his own pockets. Accordingly, for the first month of the French occupation of Madras, its future was shaped not by any effective British resistance but rather by an internecine struggle over which direction French designs on the region might take.

Clive, for his part, looked upon the whole series of events at Fort St. George with disgust. The unexpected cowardice and indiscipline of the regular troops stationed at the fort were appalling enough. But the real outrage, of course, was that the hated French had rather easily put paid to what Clive and his colleagues had begun not so long before to make their life's business. If nothing changed, then these young company servants would soon be carted off to Pondicherry, there likely to be repatriated to Britain as pawns in a geostrategic game, their careers over. After a month of what they regarded as a humiliating parole, the first glimmers of a way forward arrived with the monsoon rains. The rains' unmistakable advent induced the now vulnerable French fleet to attempt a departure to calmer waters. In the event, the monsoon's ferocious impact was a disaster for la Bourdonnais's fleet: four ships foundered and sank, one was dismasted, while another was blown off its course, eventually making port at Ceylon.

In witnessing this catastrophe for the French, Clive and three of his fellow writer colleagues were emboldened to defy their captors. Despite François Dupleix having arrived to exert his gubernatorial authority over the situation and to remove former English governor

Morse and the garrison's senior officers and company servants to Pondicherry, Clive and his group refused to give their word that they would not raise arms against the remaining French-occupying force, nor foreswear attempting to escape. The French seemed to not be overly fussed by this show of youthful bravado, however, and even though Clive and his companions were placed under guard, it was a rather lax form of incarceration. Accordingly, they immediately began to plan their escape, the key to which would be their decision to masquerade as Indians by darkening their faces and arms and dressing up in local clothing provided by their bemused servants. Thus attired, and taking advantage of the fact that the sole sentry who guarded them was rather desultory in carrying out his duties, the four men stole away across the citadel amid the usual confusion and chaos of the occupied fort's parade square, and in convincing disguise they strode out through the main gate. At this point their semidaring escape became interesting. The local crowd began to notice the company foursome because of "their not being able to jabber in their language," as Clive later put it, but fortunately for them no armed Frenchmen paid the scene any attention. Within minutes the small band of escapees had moved quickly away from the fort and into the surrounding woods to safety.[11]

For the better part of a week the quartet of Clive, Mun Maskelyne, John Pybus, and John Walsh trudged southward, finally arriving at Fort St. David unarmed and still disguised as Indians. The escape and the cross-country trek that followed had been audacious acts, and their welcome at the company's small remaining southern outpost was fulsome. The company's prospects were precarious at this particular moment, of course, and Clive, technically since his appointment had been at Fort St. George, was unemployed. But rather than sign on to become a temporary writer at Fort St. David, however, he chose to enlist in the military service of the company. This decision was made without the slightest inkling of its long-range importance. The pressing times faced by the company simply convinced Clive that he would be in a better position to help its cause by marching rather than by returning to the counting house.

To this end, and after some rudimentary training, he would be tested in December 1746 when the French, under Dupleix, attempted to overrun Fort St. David. They were repelled in part because of the assistance of the sympathetic Nawab of the Carnatic and his elephant-riding commander-son, Muhammad Ali. Clive's role, as a raw recruit, was minimal to nonexistent in this attack, but by the time the persistent Dupleix launched his next one, in March 1747, Clive was in the thick of it firing readily into the French lines, the number of enemy troops exceeding by a factor of two that which the British could bring to bear on the desperate situation. But just as sea power—in the form of the French fleet's departure in the teeth of the seasonal monsoon that had altered the course of events at Madras in October of the previous year—it made the difference again at Fort St. David. Only this time it was the arrival of the British fleet sailing south from Bengal that proved decisive. In view of the complete turning of the tables that such a naked show of force demonstrated, Dupleix directed the withdrawal of French forces, and they duly fell back on Pondicherry, sent there amid the raucous cheers of the British. Clive, whose escape from Fort St. George and subsequent enlistment in the company's army had made him a person of note, came out of this episode in a strong position. The governor, John Hinde, informed the Court of Directors in London that "Mr Robert Clive, Writer in the Service, being of a Martial Disposition, and having acted as a Volunteer upon our Late Engagement, we have granted him an Ensign's Commission upon his application for the same."[12]

Despite the successful British resistance at Fort St. David, Dupleix was not about to give up on his aspiration to make the French paramount in South India. Still, moving out successfully from Madras was not possible as long as the British were able to hold Fort St. David. Indeed, a stalemate set in for the remainder of 1747. At the beginning of the following year the British position was made stronger with the arrival of Maj. Stringer Lawrence at Fort St. David. A rotund, fiery officer with twenty years' experience in the British army in Spain, Flanders, and Scotland, he came to the East India Company assigned with the task of shoring up military command along the Coromandel Coast. Known later as the father of the Indian Army, Lawrence quickly moved to professionalize his mix of British and Indian troops, in the process winning their respect and admiration, as well as the fighting nickname, the Old Cock.

Lawrence's impact, together with the arrival several months later in July of Adm. Edward Boscawen and a squadron of six ships of the line, a number of other craft, and some eight hundred marines, made the British impregnable at Fort St. David. Their newfound strength also tempted them to contemplate an attack on Pondicherry, with a view to breaking the French there, from which a ready reoccupation of Madras could then be made. The plan was sensible, if grand, but bitterly for the British its execution could not have gone any worse than it did. To reach Pondicherry, a small French-fortified outpost nearby had to first be breached. It was not. In fact, in trying to take it, Major Lawrence was captured and taken as a prisoner to Pondicherry: a significant battlefield prize for the French. The main attack now fell to Boscawen, whose expertise, unsurprisingly, lay more clearly at sea than on land. In eventually laying siege to Pondicherry he incorrectly positioned his gun batteries, a mistake exacerbated by the heavy rains that rendered the ground a black soup. By October, and with the monsoon to arrive shortly, Boscawen decided to lift the siege, the ambitious plan of seizing Pondicherry ending with it.[13] Later, Clive would opine, "How very ignorant of war we were in those days."[14] The Anglo-French stalemate in South India thus would continue, although not for long as the recent cessation of the War of the Austrian Succession in Europe yielded the treaty of Aix-la-Chapelle that year. News of the war's end did not reach the Coromandel Coast until 1749, however, but when it did, the treaty's provisions included a return of Madras to British control.

Effected in August that year, the rendition of Madras meant a return to the city of Clive, whose sterling conduct in the aborted siege of Pondicherry had yielded yet more high praise—especially that concerning his holding firm with his platoon in the face of withering French fire, thereby forcing the enemy to withdraw.[15] His reward was promotion to lieutenant. If until that point Clive had been a company writer in the guise of a man of the sword, Pondicherry changed all that. He was now first and foremost a soldier with, as Lawrence would soon admiringly point out, a touch of "genius" about him.[16] The twenty-three-year-old Robert Clive was on his way.

# Emergence of the Military Leader

B Y THE END OF THE 1740s the decaying state of the
Mughal Empire offered clear opportunities for both the British and
the French to consolidate their commercial and political positions in
India. Indeed, since the death in 1707 of Aurangzeb, considered the
last of the great Mughal rulers, the empire was viewed as ripe for easy
exploitation—similar to the way in which the Ottoman Empire would
be seen as the vulnerable "sick man of Europe" by Britain and France
in the late-nineteenth and early-twentieth centuries.[1] For the East
India Company the place that its suzerainty might be imposed most
readily and comprehensively was South India, where, if it could strike
hard at the French, regional pre-eminence could be achieved.[2]

In 1748, the same year that peace in Europe was restored following
the War of the Austrian Succession, Nasir Jang, the nizam of Hyderabad,
died, setting off an Anglo-French contest over who might succeed him.
In this era of "subimperialism" in India, the British and the French could
and did fight proxy wars involving Indian enemies or clients in order to
best their European rival. To this end, for the next six years until 1754,
the so-called Carnatic War was fought, with the singular prize of being
control of the throne in Hyderabad, along with the subsidiary nawabship
of Arcot and the trading monopoly that would flow from it.

Clive's role as the company's chief military champion in the years of the Carnatic War had something of an unlikely start, however. Initially, after the peace of Aix-la-Chapelle in 1748, Clive remained at Fort St. David before his eventual return to Madras. While resident there he lodged just outside the fort at Bandlipollam in a bungalow, that functional low-rise dwelling that would enter into both the English language and Western architecture in the years to come. A brief period of quiescence settled over Clive and the fort in this period, broken only by an unlikely, though nasty, row between the young company man of arms and the fort's dyspeptic and debauched company chaplain, the Reverend Francis Fordyce. Provoked especially by reports of the chaplain's wild musings about the soldiers' "cowardice" during the company's unsuccessful struggle for Pondicherry, Clive encountered Fordyce in the street at Cuddalore, the town that sat next to the fort. Words were exchanged, the tone and content of which sparked a fight between the two men, and they struck each other with their walking sticks. Outraged by this assault on both his person and his dignity, Fordyce vowed to report the incident to the local company Council, blaming Clive for its unseemly slide into physical violence. The case was indeed heard, but Clive was wholly exonerated with the added victory for him of seeing the despised clergyman dismissed from the company's service. If not exactly a military triumph, the incident showed Clive to be no blind respecter of persons and quite happy to call out those who would attempt to slander him or his colleagues.[3]

For Clive, this tawdry street fight with an unlikely belligerent cleric would be quickly forgotten, however, when the prospect of a real military operation came into view. And such did happen in March 1749 when the British decided to act upon their aspiration to push out the French in the region. The contest to replace the nizam and the nawab was beginning to divide along predictable national lines: for the former, the British supported Muhammad Ali Walajah, while the French backed Chanda Sahib; for the latter, Nasir Jang was the British choice with Muzaffar Jang receiving the endorsement of the French. An element of gamesmanship is clear in the way in which this rivalry was pursued, with notice being given first by the British with a spring-time offensive against the tiny kingdom of Tanjore. Located south of Fort St. David, Tanjore had fallen under French suzerainty in 1739, its uncooperative ruling rajah being replaced by one ready and willing to endorse its new European overlord. The British expedition, in which the newly promoted Lieutenant Clive was given command of a company, fairly exuded hubris in the apparent expectation of an easy victory. Operationally, it was a disaster, however, because the initial troops (including Clive's) that marched south were unable to link up later with reinforcements arriving across a wildly stormy sea. Exacerbating this small force's problems was finally encountering an army of considerably greater numbers than its own. The sight of them grouped en masse left Clive "a little staggered."[4] In light of their being overmatched, the British wisely chose to retreat but did so in such a chaotic manner that their baggage train was mostly lost and hundreds of Indian bearers were drowned upon crossing a swollen river.

Despite the ignominy of this first Tanjore expedition, the promise of the territory's trade and possession of its key fort at Devakottai prompted a potentially redemptive second attempt. The outcome would prove to be exactly what Clive and his like-minded colleagues had hoped for. The main difference in this second foray was that its leadership was assumed by Stringer Lawrence. Still smarting over his earlier capture and the inability of the British to take Pondicherry, Lawrence summarily told the first expedition's commander, Capt. James Cope, to retire after which he himself led the whole garrison of Fort St. David southward and then up the Coleroon River to a site just across from Devakottai. From there, the success of the mission was left up to Clive. As he was Lawrence's favorite, Clive's request to lead the assault party was granted, and with thirty British troops backed by seven hundred Indian *sepoys* (from the Persian word for soldier, as native troops were now routinely called) Clive charged ahead. In so doing he exhibited plenty of bravado, to be sure, but also a touch of foolhardiness. Once having advanced across the river, or *nullah*, to a position not far from the fort, Clive was mortified to find that he had outrun his sepoys and was now exposed to a direct enemy attack. He had no support to the rear. Instantly, his precarious position was exploited by an onrush of previously hidden enemy cavalry, who descended upon Clive's small band of men, swords raised, slashing and cutting until all but a handful of British troops were left standing— Clive among them.

Across the river, a horrified Lawrence had witnessed this close call and was quick to spur the supporting sepoys to cross the river and draw up in front of the fort, causing the Tanjore troops to pull back. From there, with Lawrence in command, and with the whole body of his troops arranged for the purpose, victory came swiftly. The enemy army, still in enormous numbers totaling perhaps fifteen thousand, were nonetheless undisciplined and broke and ran, abandoning the fort. Why the Tanjore army did so is not clear, but to the victorious British it was evidence that a concentrated and unrelenting attack was the key to overcoming any "oriental" opponent. In any event, the old and now pro-British rajah was reinstalled, and the victory was complete. So too was Clive's own when Lawrence chose yet again to heap praise on his conduct by later writing: "This young man's early genius surprised and engaged my attention, as well before the siege of Devikottai, where he behaved in courage and judgement much beyond what could be expected from his years."[5]

Lawrence's words of praise were then followed up with action. He appointed Clive his quartermaster, or steward, which was potentially a highly lucrative post and a clear demonstration of his personal patronage of the young company warrior. Clive then accompanied his patron to Madras, stopping en route at Pondicherry, where he met the redoubtable French governor, François Dupleix. Despite the late British surge, Dupleix remained supremely confident of the French position relative to that of the British; indeed, much more was required to declare victory in South India than the rather small engagement at Devakottai. Nevertheless, success there boded well for both Clive and the company.

Once having arrived in Madras, however, Clive found his military life beginning to wane. The first cause was that the governor, Charles Floyer, and council were wearying of the cost of protracted warfare and somewhat dubious (notwithstanding the victory at Devakottai) of its efficacy in expanding regional trade; after all, the recent peace had restored the trading situation status quo antebellum in Europe. Madras itself was in a state of abandonment and disrepair, and needed to be rebuilt, regarrisoned, and reprovisioned. Secondly, however, was the rapid impact that Clive's appointment as steward was having on his own financial position. Indeed, it is to this period that the initial accumulation of Clive's great wealth can be traced. Important too, in Clive's thinking about a military future at this point, was his keen disappointment over the fact that his application for promotion to captain had been denied by the Court of Directors, an endorsement of the Fort St. George Council's decision to reduce the company's military expenditures.[6]

In the meantime, Clive returned to his ledger books, only this time each transaction carried with it a tidy personal commission to which he was entitled as steward. The job was significant, the turnover large. Clive was responsible for every supply required by the fort: beef, pork, tobacco, oil for lamps, alcohol—especially in the form of arrack, the Indian liquor to which each company servant and soldier was entitled, and more. On all of it, he could legitimately levy a charge of 5 to 10 percent. If still put out about his inability to rise any higher in the company's army, Clive could at least take satisfaction in the steadily increasing size of his purse. Not even a protracted bout of typhoid fever, which necessitated a few months' spent convalescing in the relatively cooler climate to the north at Fort William (Calcutta), could alter that. Indeed, if anything, the somewhat grander and more European-style Calcutta convinced Clive that his original aspiration to succeed in trade could be met more readily by a transfer there. Accordingly, he applied for such in the spring of 1750 after having returned to Madras. But the transfer was turned down on account of his continuing position of steward. Regardless, Clive's first experience of Calcutta and Bengal had reoriented his thinking, and the two locals would soon enough alter his life.

In addition to making him think that perhaps he should move north, Clive's period in Calcutta had resulted also in acquiring a close friend, Robert Orme. Born in India to a physician at the small East India Company settlement of Anjengo, Orme was sent to London as a young child to be educated. After seven years at Harrow School, the classically educated Orme returned to India at the age of thirteen and shortly thereafter made a writer in the company's service at Calcutta. Apparently discontented with the rather rote work, he became deeply engaged in the study of Britain's impact on Indian society, a pursuit that would eventually yield a serious work of contemporary scholarship, *History of the Military Transactions of the British Nation in Indostan*

(1763–1778).[7] Clive was greatly impressed by the young Orme's erudition, as well as by his sophistication, and they struck up an immediate friendship; later, Orme's prolific pen would do much to establish Clive's reputation as the key figure in the company's expansion in Bengal in the mid-1750s.

In the meantime, having returned to Madras in renewed health, Clive plunged back into his work as steward. The remainder of the year 1750 would find him "chin deep in merchandize" and plainly unengaged in any military pursuits.[8] But such were never far away, as the French under Dupleix continued to be restive.

French forwardness turned to concerted action when in December 1750 Dupleix's machinations resulted in the murder of Nasir Jang, the British-backed contender to be the new nizam of Hyderabad. His killing was a sharp example of realpolitik, propelling the French candidate, Muzaffar Jang, into power as nizam, and thereby making it clear to the British that they had been bested in the local power struggle. The new governor at Madras, Thomas Saunders was, however, unlike his predecessor Floyer in that he was made of sterner stuff and was planning very keenly to check the French. After Saunders took up his appointment in September, Nasir Jang was pitilessly murdered just three months later, an act that he found deeply offensive in its brutality but that also opened the way for him to attempt to counter the French. The British chose to do so beginning in May 1751 when they lent support to the continuing campaign of their client Muhammad Ali Walajah to claim the nizam's throne by sending a force to defend him at his redoubt of Trichinopoly. In the event, the campaign was a disaster, occasioned mainly by the fact that Stringer Lawrence had left Madras in a foul state of mind to return to England. The company's directors—having chosen to demonstrate their continuing parsimony in concert with the local council by cutting his salary in half—got what they deserved in that the new officer chosen by Saunders to lead the expedition, a Swiss mercenary captain named Rudolph de Guingens, proved unable to do so effectively. The military result of this failed foray to Trichinopoly was that the British force ended up merely holding it, while their enemy under the command of Chanda Sahib, the French-backed candidate to become the nizam, encamped his enormous army outside the city and waited for its expected surrender.

For Clive, the Trichinopoly fiasco was aggravating. His role in the expedition extending from his position as steward was to run the commissariat. He did so without much enthusiasm, stemming both from his frustration at being indirectly involved in such fighting as there was and from the ignominious way in which his champion, Lawrence, had earlier departed for England. There was little by which to commend the British in their current state, cowering—or so it seemed—behind the walls of Trichinopoly. In a highly agitated state of mind, Clive left the besieged city with some like-minded colleagues and rode by horseback to Fort St. David, there to consult with the transplanted Governor Saunders about taking certain steps that might reverse the impending loss of Trichinopoly and with it yet another victory for the French.

Once having arrived at Fort St. David, Clive offered himself as a volunteer in the company army, but only on the condition that he be made a captain. Saunders, chastened by the failure of his handpicked Swiss mercenary to win the day at Trichinopoly, was quick to say yes and to give him his requested rank. Clive then was sent swiftly back to the imperiled Trichinopoly with a detachment of men, and while there he discussed with Muhammad Ali Walajah what might be done to break the stalemate that had settled over the British and Chanda Sahib. The plan that Walajah had been considering and which he now shared with Clive was one of marching a British force to Arcot, the capital of the Carnatic, and by so doing surprise Chanda Sahib in his seat of government. The rationale was that Arcot at this point was only lightly defended since the bulk of its garrison was encamped in front of Trichinopoly. If successful, an attack on Arcot might very well cripple Chanda and thereby Muzaffar Jang too, catching them out and exposing their weakness in defending their regional capital city. Arcot, located only sixty-five miles almost directly inland from Madras, was a fairly easy march for the British, and the possibility of falling upon its unsuspecting denizens by surprise was high. To both Walajah and Clive, and then in due course Saunders, the probability of victory was clear and with it so too was the potential for inflicting a severely damaging blow on the French.

Initially, however, Saunders would show little perspicacity in deciding that the hapless de Guingens should lead this proposed expedition.

But the Swiss captain, still stinging from his inability to achieve anything positive from his march on Trichinopoly, rather petulantly, one suspects, told Saunders that success along the lines envisaged at Arcot was impossible. Confirming his increasingly critical estimation of the man, however, Saunders was now ready to listen to alternatives of who might be able to command a force that would succeed in taking Arcot. In so doing he handed leadership of the expedition over to Clive. Just back from Trichinopoly, Captain Clive had argued hard for the chance to lead the mission and got it. The assignment was highly fortuitous, as Arcot would prove to be the making of him militarily.

Arcot had a population of about a hundred thousand. As a capital, it certainly was not grand, but it was well located along the Palar River on the heavily traveled trade route from Madras to Bangalore. The city sat at the foot of the Javadi Hills with the towering mountains of the Mysore Ghat visible in the background, while in front of it was spread out the dusty expanse of the Choultry Plain. In Clive's moving decisively on Trichinopoly, it was understood that Chanda Sahib had left Arcot with a depleted garrison. But the city was far from defenseless, as Clive would discover soon enough. At Fort St. David, under Governor Saunders's direction, Clive received his initial troop strength for the expeditionary force. Amounting to about 120 British soldiers, along with some sepoys, this band of fighters then sailed briefly north to Madras where an additional eighty British regulars were added to their number, as well as additional sepoys, whose field pay was low but regular to ensure loyalty. The combined strength of Clive's forces totaled some 200 British troops along with about 500 sepoys, and on the morning of August 26, 1751, Clive's 700-man army set out on foot for Arcot, most armed with swords and flintlock muskets.

The march was hot and dusty. The scarlet tunics of the company's soldiers stood out sharply against the brown scrub of the plain. Sweat poured down the faces of the troops, British and Indian alike. Despite their crisp uniforms and the company's imprimatur, this army was not especially professional, however. Indeed, many years later Clive would speak disparagingly of these and all company troops of this early period simply as "scum."[9] Hindsight may have given him the license to do so; contemporary requirements did not. Scum or no, Clive would need every one of them if he were to succeed in this attack on the capital city of the Carnatic. Dragging along three small field guns, Clive's men marched at a rate of about fifteen miles per day, plodding along in the oppressive heat and humidity of the South Indian summer until reaching Conjeevaram, the first major town en route, located about a day's march from Arcot. Here, Clive was informed that even though Chanda Sahib had drawn off thousands of troops from Arcot in his attempt to take Trichinopoly, the city remained fairly well defended, perhaps by as many as a thousand men. The news spurred Clive to request that Madras send him some additional field guns immediately. The deputy governor there, Richard Prince, who was highly supportive of the expedition from the beginning, sent an immediate reply promising to do so.[10]

Clive was impatient now, keen to attack Arcot and make a success of this bold and—hopefully to its defenders—surprising mission. With Prince's promised guns acting as a spur, he pushed his tired men on for the last few miles to the city through a terrific storm, arriving at its outskirts on September 1. By the time Clive's sodden band arrived at Arcot's gates, the garrison and the city's inhabitants had known for a few days that they were coming, the news having been relayed by Chanda Sahib's scouts. Indeed, such was the apparent daring of the British force marching through the thunder, lightning, and downpour that the thousand or so men who were supposed to be guarding the city had become entirely unnerved by the prospect of these miraculous foreigners and fled a few miles into the countryside. Who were they to defy the gods in a land where typically nobody fought in the rain?[11]

In any event, Clive and his troops entered Arcot unopposed, the city's inhabitants staring out wide-eyed at the invaders from inside their tumbledown buildings, but nonresistant. In a span of five days Clive had pulled off a daring feat of arms without firing a single shot. Leading hundreds of troops for the first time in a cross-country operation, Clive had demonstrated a clear capacity to command both European regulars and non-European irregulars and sepoys, and a bullish desire to succeed. The British could not afford any additional military failures if South India were to be prevented from falling completely under French influence, and his rapid march had given the British the initiative: Arcot was Clive's, at least for the moment. But so as not to give the unwelcome impression to the locals that a British conquest had occurred, Clive ran up the flag of Muhammad Ali Walajah, and while the reassuringly traditional Islamic colors of green and white snapped in the morning breeze he contemplated what to do next.

Clive had several options to consider. He could stay put and prepare for a siege that he assumed would come as soon as Chanda Sahib had turned his full attention to the situation in Arcot and away from Trichinopoly. He could scatter his troops regionally and hope to undermine Chanda's country position even further. He could lay waste to the place and retire to Madras having struck a highly damaging blow that could be exploited later and elsewhere. In finding himself in the somewhat unbelievable position of being the keeper of Arcot, the young Clive (who would turn twenty-six years of age later that month) was having an entirely understandable moment of indecision. Back at Fort St. David, however, Governor Saunders displayed no such irresolution. He was sure that holding onto the city and then confronting Chanda's troops with a view to breaking him was the right course. After all, so far in this rather hasty expedition everything had gone right, and it could only be hoped that such luck would continue. Clive quickly became of the same mind as Saunders and began to closely consider his position and to stockpile supplies by which to withstand a siege.

To begin, the fort at Arcot was old, dilapidated in places, and about a mile in circumference, outside of which lay the city, a dark and dusty warren of houses, shops, temples, and pagodas. Many of the fort's battlements were crumbling, as were its towers. The fort was ringed by a moat, but it too was in poor condition. The likelihood of the moat being forded in one or more places was high. The possibility of a force of just seven hundred men securing a fort the size of Arcot's was low. In all, Clive and his men faced a very difficult task. Wishing to stave off an attack on his vulnerable redoubt, Clive initially took the battle to the enemy by leading a couple of probing forays to the nearby encampment of Chanda's men who had previously garrisoned the fort. By this point the number of men Clive had at his disposal had tripled to about three thousand, bolstered by reinforcements coming in from Trichinopoly to the south. On September 14, two weeks after taking Arcot, Clive launched a surprise piercing movement in the middle of the night that cut through the encamped former garrison. The terrifying attack had the right effect, for by the time the sun rose a few hours later the enemy had dispersed. This move bought Clive some time, and shortly thereafter the artillery pieces Prince had promised arrived, although to get them to Arcot safely Clive would have to send hundreds of his men to escort the convoy from Conjeevaram. In so doing, the fort's defenses were seriously undermanned, but still Clive's forces did prevail.

In relative security now preparations for a full siege continued apace. Clive was sure that Chanda would have been in contact with Dupleix, during which presumably the promise of French support would be made plain. Chanda's younger son and commander, Raza Sahib, indeed had been in close consultation with the French governor, and on September 23 a force of some 150 French soldiers, together with at least 4,000 Indian troops, began to invest the city. The strength of and preparations made by Clive and his men were now about to be fully tested.

The arrival of the enemy in such numbers, swarming through the city, had the unsurprising impact of spooking Clive and his badly outnumbered men. In desperation, Clive directed them to leave their fortified positions and go on the offensive. A wild firefight thus ensued in which a number of French gunners were killed, but so too were at least fifteen of Clive's own British troops, some 10 percent of their total number. Luckily, Clive himself escaped being shot, a musket ball missing him narrowly but killing the lieutenant who had tugged him hard to safety. Indeed, fighting in the dust of Arcot's streets was a foolhardy business, and Clive soon realized it. If his men were to have any chance at all in this lopsided encounter, they would have to roll up the ramparts and hope that the siege could be endured until a relief force might arrive.

By the end of September, Clive and his force were in full siege mode. Clive passed his birthday in this way, amid a force that consisted now of only some 120 British troops along with about 200 sepoys. It was a reduction in size brought on by both the steady drip-drip of casualties and by having to send some of his men back to Madras to bolster its weakened defenses in case Raza Sahib should decide to divert part of his burgeoning force and launch an attack there. Indeed,

Raza's numbers were increasing steadily and would top out eventually at over seven thousand men. In terms of manpower alone, Clive's situation looked correspondingly hopeless. But in other ways he and his three hundred or so men were in a reasonably strong position to withstand what looked to be a protracted siege. Their food supply was plentiful, with enough to last at least three months or more. Likewise, the fort's water reservoir was full and, because its channel had been blocked up from the inside, could not be drained by the enemy. Clive's supply of powder and shot was also large. All in all, the besieged Anglo-Indian force could be expected to put up a terrific resistance for at least a few months. The men, especially the British, of course found the temperatures unbearably hot, well over a hundred degrees in the shade, and the humidity of the air heavy and close. Heatstroke occurred, and men looked on in disgust as heat boils broke out on their arms and legs. The fact that despite the presence of thousands of the enemy outside the fort's walls no serious breach had yet occurred heartened them all.

Constant sentry duty, however, was greatly tiring. And the mental strain of being always on edge sapped the strength of the men too. Clive lived in a perpetually heightened state. He patrolled the walls along with his men, on several occasions narrowly avoiding the steady musket fire that emerged from the windows and doorways of the streets and laneways that ringed the fort. Wary of the British firepower and also cowed by the symbolism of Chanda's capital having fallen to them, Raza's troops made no attempt to storm the fort, being content instead to fire steadily on those targets that appeared along the walls.

Meanwhile, Clive was in regular communication with Saunders and Prince about the arrival date and size of the relief force. In classic fashion he made use of a series of surreptitious couriers who were able to slip in and out of the fort, passing through the occupied city in much the same way that Gen. Charles Gordon would later employ them famously in 1884 during the Mahdi's siege of Khartoum.[12] Accordingly, a courier brought word to Clive that a small force of perhaps two hundred men in total was coming, but its arrival could not be expected before the end of October. Clive would have to carry on at least until then. In the meantime, the enemy's emplacement of some French artillery pieces had made that task even more difficult. Their deployment and a week-long bombardment meant that the fort's walls were indeed breached, but a new entrenched line of defense was hurriedly constructed and the enemy could not gain entry. Back and forth went whizzing projectiles, Clive's two eighteen-pound guns firing away, with Raza's new French guns answering in like manner. Clive was even able to restore an old Mughal cannon found inside the fort, which he then used to pound the gun positions of the enemy. Included in this assault was the sport of lobbing cannonballs into the nawab's palace, which Raza and his French colleagues used as a command post.

Despite such adaptations, Clive's position remained dire. The men were exhausted, both physically and mentally. Indeed, Clive later cited fatigue as being more to be feared than the enemy.[13] By early November the siege was well into its second month. Saunders's promised relief force had not yet arrived. The supplies that had once been plentiful were now just beginning to deplete. But as so often happened in Indian warfare of the time, an unexpected development quickly changed the status quo. The Hindu Marathas, a long-standing enemy of Chanda, had been enlisted by the Regent of Mysore to aid Muhammad Ali Walajah in his quest to become nizam. Massed under the command of Morari Rao, a legendary fighter, six thousand Marathi warriors were poised in anticipation of defending the fort while the regent negotiated with Walajah the terms by which he would agree to march on Arcot and give relief to the beleaguered Clive and his men.[14] The threat of six thousand Marathi soldiers descending upon the city prompted Raza to offer terms of surrender to Clive. Emboldened, however, by the possibility of the arrival of the Marathas, as well as by the prospect of the promised British relief force from Madras, Clive dismissed the offer as contemptible. In the event, Raza had no choice but to launch an attack, which he did on the morning of November 14.

The storming of Arcot is one of the archetypal set-pieces of European-Indian warfare of this era. Mid-November meant that the Muslim celebration of Mohurrum, the ten-day period of fasting and mourning for the martyrdom of the Prophet Muhammad's grandson, Hussein, reached its climax. Raza's soldiers were principally Muslims of the Shi'a variety, meaning that in marking this particular Muslim rite, they were spoiling for a fight and were frenzied in doing so. As usual in such situations both then and now, the promise of an immediate passage to heaven for killing the infidel brought with it a terrific martial surge.

On came Chanda's men, therefore, shrieking, shooting, and carrying siege ladders, led by spectacularly arrayed war elephants, protected—it was assumed—by their facial plate armor. Such a sight was indeed formidable, but almost immediately Clive commanded his men to shoot the elephants where no armor protected them.[15] They did so, and in a scene that might be thought of as similar to Zama fifteen centuries earlier in BC 202 when Hannibal's elephants had broken and stampeded against their Carthaginian handlers in the onrush of the Romans under Scipio Africanus, Raza's terrified and wounded elephants did the same.

The scattering of the war elephants portended a wider dispersal of the attacking troops. Their target, the main gate of the fort, which survives to this day and within its upper room Clive had held strategy meetings during the siege, held fast. Elsewhere, where breaches had been made earlier in the walls by French guns, the wild-eyed enemy did meet with a small amount of success. Indeed, one of Raza's commanders, Abdul Khan, made it through the wall, crossed the moat, and quickly planted the enemy flag. But within seconds he was picked off by a musketeer. Khan's death seemed to dishearten the attacking troops, and as their zeal slackened, Raza decided to withdraw, effectively conceding defeat.[16]

The storming of the fort had cost Raza some three hundred men, with nothing to show for it. The dead soldiers' bodies lay strewn in front of the fort, their dichotomous impact on the morale of both sets of fighters palpable. In the face of the carnage suffered by Raza's troops, only four British soldiers had fallen, along with a mere two sepoys wounded. The defense of the fort was a ringing success; in barely sixty minutes' worth of fighting the enemy had been routed. Raza did take the next few hours to regroup and launch a barrage that Clive thought might be a softening-up exercise in advance of a second assault. In fact, Raza knew already that the day was lost, something soon confirmed by the arrival of the British relief force from Madras and the nearby encampment of the Marathas. His barrage had actually been cover-fire designed to allow his troops to withdraw. After fifty-two days the siege of Arcot was over. Clive and his men had done more than survive, they had triumphed. And most importantly for East India Company fortunes, the French in their supplementary role had been handed a stinging defeat.

As important as the triumph at Arcot would prove to be—"your brave conduct and success which providence has blest you with is the talk and wonder of the publick, the great joy and satisfaction of all your friends," as Rebecca Clive would write later to her son—like most events in military history its larger significance was not immediately apparent to either the victor or the loser.[17] Indeed, in its aftermath, the fighting continued because while Arcot was a stunning, if protracted, victory for Clive and the company, the region itself remained highly contested in the ongoing struggle between the British and the French for supremacy.

Thus less than three weeks later Clive was back in martial mode, this time near the small town of Arni, about twenty miles south of Arcot. Raza Sahib's army, having retired to nearby Vellore, had been joined by further French reinforcements, and on the morning of December 3, 1751, the two armies met. Clive's forces had been supplemented by the Marathas under Morari Rao, who had finally been convinced that the price offered for their participation indeed was high enough. Together their victory at Arni came swiftly. Clive and his new allies made short work of Raza's men, the victory here being Clive's first in the field, as distinct from that at Arcot of resisting a siege. So thorough was the triumph that hundreds of enemy sepoys sought to come over to Clive's side, abandoning the French who they deemed to be incompetent in both command and execution. Clive happily accepted many of them, and in so doing he believed that on the evidence provided by the combination of victories at Arcot and Arni the British position had been solidified enough to allow for the declaration of a regional victory, and for him to happily return to Madras.

He did not, however, end up quitting the field just yet, urged not to be "too hasty" by Governor Saunders, but rather to stay on and flush out the French from nearby Conjeevaram.[18] Going on to do exactly that by mid-December, Clive then indeed did return to Madras and to Fort St. David, welcomed in both places as a conquering hero. If nothing else, however, the Carnatic War would demand persistence. Raza and the French continued to harass the British whenever an opportunity presented itself. They knew—as assuredly did Clive— that without the help of the Marathas, who had decided that they had scored enough from this campaign for the time being and therefore had dispersed, the company was not nearly as strong as it needed to be to stave off Raza's ready imprecations.

To that end, Clive and Saunders began to strategize and to do everything possible to build up a proper army, one that hopefully could break Raza and the French completely. Indeed, by early 1752 such an army had been cobbled together, consisting of some four hundred British troops and thirteen hundred sepoys. Such numbers made Clive's force comparable to what Raza could now put in the field, but with Clive sporting at least a ten-to-one advantage in his British troops to Raza's French ones. After brief preliminaries, the two armies met near the village of Kaveripak, located about ten miles east of Arcot, on February 28. For Clive, the encounter got off to a rather bad start, however, as near the end of a day's march, and in the approaching dusk, his army found itself unexpectedly stumbling into Raza's camp. They came under fire almost immediately, the impact of the French guns pinning down Clive's men. A stalemate ensued, maintained by reciprocal musket and artillery fire. In this fitful two-hour engagement Raza's troops gradually gained the upper hand until Clive was advised by a subordinate that there was a way to surreptitiously approach Raza's position from the rear. Acting on this advice Clive sent a detachment of two hundred men to silently approach Raza's troops. In this way when they had crept up to within a mere fifty yards of the enemy they fired a volley into the rear of their lines. Almost immediately, the surprised and panicked French and sepoy troops broke and ran; within an hour Clive was simply mopping up. Kaveripak was his, although the cost to his army on the day was not inconsiderable: some seventy killed, the number about evenly split between British troops and sepoys.

Kaveripak was another impressive victory for Clive. His win there had the effect of disbanding Raza's troops and making the British supreme in the area and thereby cementing the political position of their client Muhammad Ali Walajah. Arcot, Arni, and Kaveripak—three victories in a row—did the same for Clive's reputation, and the march back to Fort St. David was a celebratory one, punctuated by an almost gleeful (and clearly less than magnanimous) putting to the torch the town of Dupleix Fatihabad, the place where a little over a year earlier Nasir Jang had been murdered on the orders of the eponymous French governor. Upon completing this victorious trek and reaching Fort St. David, Clive was met unexpectedly but happily by Stringer Lawrence, freshly returned from London.

The last prize in what had become a quartet of redoubts that had to be taken to truly stand atop the French in South India was Trichinopoly, located about 150 miles west of Fort St. David. Clive, naturally emboldened by his run of victories, was keen to march on it and, with a victory, properly smash the French and the hated François Dupleix. The "Old Cock," Lawrence, was equally keen to move on Trichinopoly, and once in command he made Clive his deputy. Together, Lawrence and Clive made a rather intimidating pair of British warlords. The siege of Trichinopoly as it began in March 1752 was one of the largest of the Anglo-French wars in South India. By the time the British-led force approached the city on March 29, it had a total strength of some forty thousand men to about thirty thousand for the enemy. To the redcoats could be added Muhammad Ali Walajah's thousands of troops, Morari Rao's fierce Marathas—back for more after a short hiatus—plus soldiers supplied by the regents of Mysore and Tanjore, both of whom were betting on the British emerging triumphant in this struggle of European powers. In opposition stood Dupleix, directing French operations from Pondicherry, and in the field Chanda Sahib along with a Franco-Scots commander, Jacques Law. Both of these massive armies were unruly and shambling, however, moving organisms of arms and men, elephants and horses (sometimes camels too), with thousands of camp followers comprising family members, wallahs (servants) of various sorts, and the inevitable "nautch" girls, the ever-present prostitutes who were as much a part of Indian military life as its infantry or cavalry. Most of the time these colorful military amalgams moved slowly, but if panicked they could become swift and swirling in motion and as dangerous to those caught up in their midst as to the enemy waiting in fearful opposition.

As befit the two armies' size, however, their first clash at Trichinopoly was spectacular in its execution. Chanda Sahib's cannons were unleashed against a surprised Lawrence, who nonetheless quickly steadied his troops before moving forward at a measured pace, the beat of the drums ensuring uniformity in martial gait. The flat expanse in front of Trichinopoly quickly was turned into a kind of medieval battleground of banners, pikes, spears, and men, the distinctively Indian feature of it being the war elephants on which commanders rode in an inspiring, though for many fatally, conspicuous position. The great guns of each side pounded away in reciprocal murderous fire. Meanwhile, as this set-piece battle proceeded, Clive stole away in order to find a protected place where the British forces might make a stand. He found it in the existence of a *choultry*, the ubiquitous conjoined Indian village covering. The artillery was moved there, and thus protected, the British guns continued in their fierce onslaught, an exhibition of firepower that finally drove Chanda Sahib's troops to retreat, especially so when a cannonball blew the head right off their leading commander, Allum Khan.

This first engagement allowed the British and their allies to move readily into Trichinopoly, putting Chanda Sahib and Law on the defensive, a position from which they would never really recover over the next two months. Nonetheless, once they had regrouped, the siege grew hot again in early April. By this time, however, Law had made the mistake of retreating out of the city to nearby Srirangam, a peninsula that divided two local rivers, the Cauvery and the Coleroon, the latter known by Clive from his earlier battle at Devakottai. Thus ensconced, Law hoped to resist his attackers. The first of these was Clive, who was dispatched with a force of some two thousand men to break up Law's lines of communication and encircle his walled redoubt at Srirangam. This Clive did, but then, in a move typical of the man, he exceeded his brief. Having been informed that a French relief force was approaching Srirangam, Clive decided to ambush it. Lawrence told him not to do so, but he went anyway in the middle of the night. In so doing Clive led most of his men (he had left a small detachment at Srirangam) on what amounted to a fruitless and exhausting four-hour circuit in which the French force was not intercepted. Meanwhile, while Clive was out vainly searching for the French, Law had learned of his absence and decided to launch an attack on the undermanned, at least temporarily, British position. Shortly after Clive and his men had returned from night-stalking and collapsed exhausted, Law's French forces used a captured Indian scout and a hapless British deserter to gain entry to Clive's sleeping camp. Once inside, a wild melee ensued in which Clive, attired only in his nightshirt, barely escaped death twice. The British were lucky to survive this near-farce;

most especially was Clive himself fortunate to emerge from it with nothing more than a scarred face and blood-soaked clothing. But even though he had disobeyed Lawrence, Clive's luck held and that made all the difference: "I rejoice at your success," Lawrence wrote to him, adding sardonically, "your wounds are not dangerous, and if they spoil the beauty of your face they raise your fame."[19]

Following this episode, the British regrouped and steadily pushed Chanda Sahib's forces to contract until they finally surrendered on June 4. Among the spoils taken from the defeated enemy was Raza Sahib's prize elephant, which Clive gave to Lawrence. The siege of Trichinopoly was over, and once again the British and their allies had scored a victory over the pro-French forces. The French position in South India, which in 1746 looked secure after they had taken Madras so easily, seemed now to have very nearly evaporated in the searing heat of an Indian June.

In the aftermath of the fall of Trichinopoly, Chanda Sahib was executed at the joint behest of Muhammad Ali Walajah and the Regent of Mysore. His death was swift and ignominious and clearly symbolized the emergence of the British as the reckoning power in South India. In Pondicherry, Dupleix was livid. Serial defeats by the British had taken their toll on his once glittering reputation, and in short order he was recalled to Paris, his dream of a French Indian Empire over—at least for the moment. In the meantime, Clive returned to Fort St. David and then to Madras. The military job seemingly done, he immediately hung up his sword in favor of the more lucrative and much less dangerous work of being steward. For most of the previous two years he had been a warrior, engaged fully in planning and giving battle, rallying troops, and on occasion fighting desperately for his own life. Understandably, Clive was tired. Accordingly, he settled into a rented house within Fort St. George and went back to conducting business. The profits duly rolled in—as they had done also while he was away on campaign—and by 1753 he had amassed a fortune of some £40,000, an enormous sum that would be quite sufficient to raise himself up the greasy pole of the sociopolitical structure at home in England, whenever he might return there.

As a war hero of substantial means, and a bachelor, Clive had now become a highly attractive potential husband for a reputable woman.

He was twenty-seven years of age and perfectly marriageable. He was also happily engaged in the pastime of most of his contemporaries, whether in India or England: whoring.[20] He sampled regularly the carnal delights of the Madras prostitutes, a practice he regarded as "gallanting the ladies," and which was accepted by most of his peers as normal behavior. There were few white women at any of the company settlements, and those that were in residence were married and respectable. For young men seeking sexual experience and physical release, prostitution was the only option, and it was taken up readily. Of course, the Church maintained its prohibition against premarital sexual relations, and no virginal woman seeking to maintain her reputation would allow herself to be seduced. At the same time, an adulterous affair could well lead to scandal, especially in the small and tightly knit communities that were the company presidencies. In light of these censures, therefore, whoring answered the male requirement. As a friend wrote profanely to Clive in the autumn of 1752, when the whoring life continued apace but it seemed that marriage nevertheless was in the offing: "you fuck as usual."[21]

The reason that marriage for Clive seemed likely was the arrival of Margaret Maskelyne in Madras that June. As Mun Maskelyne's younger sister, "Peggy" had come out to India with a group of similarly aged young women, all of whom were intent on marriage. Later, such groups of women arriving in India would be disparaged as members of the "fishing fleet," but such were the Georgian social strictures around respectability that apart from marrying well there were few life options for women of standing.[22] Mun Maskelyne was keen on the prospect of his not-quite seventeen-year-old sister, fresh from Wiltshire, marrying his best friend and had written home often of Clive's exploits. Mun's campaigning did its work for it is clear that Peggy arrived in Madras highly taken with the idea of Clive, if not yet with the man himself. In any event, all went to plan. They met, courted, were betrothed, and then on February 18, 1753, were married in St. Mary's Church at Fort St. George.

The wedding itself, however, seems to have come about almost impulsively. On February 15, Clive had booked a single passage to England, in what would be his first visit home in the ten years he had been in the East India Company's service. Yet just three days later he and Margaret wed, and barely a month after that, they sailed for home. There's little doubt that Clive was a happy and satisfied man as he took his leave of Madras roads, bound for London and a reunion with his family. But the previous six months had brought him not only increased wealth and a wife, they had brought him illness as well. A short military campaign had been required of Clive in September 1752. He answered the unexpected call successfully in nearby Covelong and Chingleput, the pesky French still needling the British but without the morale or the resources to cause them much damage. Clive came out of this brief engagement with two months' worth of physical complaints all the same. Fever, probably malarial, dogged him, but so too did excruciating abdominal pain and sleeplessness. To allay the pain the febrile Clive took opium, the prescribed medicine for that time and place. The drug worked its wonders, including the all-too-frequent impact of enslaving its imbibers. Clive, it seems, developed a mild addiction to opium during this period. He also fell victim to an episode of depression—a not unusual side effect of prolonged opium use—the first of many such episodes that would recur for the rest of his life. Nonetheless, despite these trials, the February nuptials were joyous, and on March 23 Captain and Mrs. Clive boarded the *Bombay Castle* and, accompanied by Robert Orme, having come south from Calcutta, departed India on the long journey home to family and friends.

Having left England a mere stripling of seventeen nearly ten years earlier, Clive was now returning home as a battle-hardened and wealthy man of twenty-seven. The reunion with his parents, Richard and Rebecca, now living in London (Clive would shortly pay off most of their mortgage on the Shropshire family seat of Styche Hall), was naturally a joyful one. After an almost-seven-month voyage Clive and his teenaged bride arrived at the East India Docks on October 10 and were soon ensconced in a rented house in Queen's Square, Ormond Street, located in moderately fashionable Bloomsbury. A visit to the company's directors was made straightaway, where Clive was feted and fussed over and shortly thereafter awarded an elaborate and expensive sword as a token of thanks for his exploits on their behalf in India. Clive's military reputation had preceded him nicely, and in the months after his arrival home he was treated as nothing less than the conquering hero and coming man.

In the midst of this period that saw Clive position himself reasonably well in London society, Margaret gave birth to a son, Edward, on March 7, 1754. Known to the family as Ned, the future Earl of Powis was the first of four boys and five girls the Clives would have in quick succession (only four of these children would survive, however). Indeed, the spring of that year was a highly important one in the life of Clive because it saw him receive an offer from the company's directors to return to Madras, in addition to which he aimed to raise his social profile by seeking election to Parliament for the borough of Mitchell in Cornwall.

Standing for one of the pair of seats in this Cornish borough was the first of Clive's two forays into electoral politics, the second and much more successful occasion coming later in 1768. In the unreformed Parliament of 1754, Mitchell was a so-called "rotten" borough comprising approximately fifty voters under the joint patronage of the Earl of Sandwich and the local squire, Thomas Scawen. They stood, however, in opposition to the governing interest led by the Duke of Newcastle, the Whig prime minister. To both Sandwich and Scawen, the lately heroic and moderately famous Clive was a good choice for them to try and vault into Parliament. The election was expected to be a genuine contest, as Clive's sponsors could be sure of the votes of only a little better than half the borough's electors. In the event, and after a personal expenditure by Clive of the large sum of nearly £5,000, April's election yielded thirty votes for him and his fellow candidate, John Stephenson, enough for the victory but not sufficient to ward off a challenge as to the outcome's legitimacy. A petition to unseat Clive and his electoral partner therefore ensued, which meant that the House of Commons became the scene of a heated political contest.

The Duke of Newcastle, as prime minister, played a pivotal role in this electoral drama because he was opposed to the Earl of Sandwich and thereby to Clive and Stephenson's victory. Up against the power of the prime minister the two neophyte Parliamentarians stood little chance of success, and after almost a year's worth of political wrangling, they were duly unseated in March 1755.[23]

By this time, however, Clive had decided already that at least his immediate future lay not in consolidating his bona fides as a gentleman politician but rather in a return to India. On March 25, the day after his formal parliamentary unseating, he signed on once again with the East India Company, this time to serve as deputy-governor of Fort St. David. Critically for Clive, the new commission also included the right to the delayed prize of the Governorship of Madras, which would be his automatically upon the retirement of its incumbent, George Pigot, expected soon. But the commission went further still. Clive would be returning as a lieutenant colonel also, making clear the idea that there was more soldiering to be done in order to propel the British to the point of uncontested supremacy over the French in South India. To that end, accompanying Clive on his return would be a force of some three hundred troops, as well as three companies of artillery.

Accordingly, Clive's departure on April 23 was a rather grand affair, punctuated by the salute of cannon. It differed from his modest first departure eleven years earlier too in that standing beside him on board the *Stretham* as it sailed away from the dockyard at Deal was his wife, Margaret. She would also be returning to India, leaving behind Edward, now just past his first birthday, and a second child, an infant boy given the name of his paternal grandfather, Richard. Separation from children was one of the prices paid by almost all those who sought careers or fortunes in India from this period until the British presence there would end in the twentieth century. But for Clive, at least, who admitted to a friend at the time that he had never suffered from a "want of ambition," it was a price well worth paying.[24]

# Battle of Plassey

T HE VOYAGE TO INDIA TOOK the usual six months with the *Stretham* carrying the Clives arriving in Bombay in late October 1755. Founded by the Portuguese, Bombay had been given to the English Crown in 1661 as part of the dowry of Catherine of Braganza, Charles II's wife.[1] Seven years later, and understandably without an ounce of sentimental attachment to this steamy unseen outpost, the king in turn gifted it to the company. Despite its apparent neglect, Bombay had prospered quickly, however, its ideal location on the west coast of the subcontinent being made even better by a good harbor. In the years after 1668 Bombay quickly displaced the older and more northerly Surat as the company's main factory in the region.

Prior to his arrival in 1755 Clive had never been to Bombay. His presence there now was in order to strike a blow at the French-backed Nizam of Hyderabad, Salabat Jang, whose power extended over the Deccan Plateau, a wide swath of territory in south-central India located directly east of Bombay. Clive had been tasked with mounting an expedition against Jang and his French client, Charles de Bussy, who had taken over command from the recently dismissed François Dupleix. The troops that had accompanied Clive from England were shortly in place for the purpose. But, in swift fashion, the company's

Bombay Council—which had turned unaccountably skittish—changed the objective from a broad attack on the Deccan to one of smashing the nearby fortress of Gheria, the redoubt of the local pirate king Tulaji Angria who had been harassing and raiding the company's ships in the region.

By Christmas, Clive was, therefore, deep into preparations to attack Gheria. He would command the company's land forces, while at sea Vice Adm. Charles Watson and Rear Adm. George Pocock would rain fire on the pirate fortress. Watson, in particular, became a good friend of Clive's during this engagement, and together they would soon move onto bigger and more important events. The son of a cleric, the hale and hearty Watson had gone to sea as a fourteen-year-old and rose steadily in the navy, becoming commander in chief on the Newfoundland and North American station in 1748. Six years later he was appointed to the same command in the East Indies, arriving in Bombay from the Coromandel Coast late in 1755.

In January of the New Year, Clive and Watson conferred, and then in early February they sailed the short distance south from Bombay to Gheria. Long thought of as an impregnable fortress in the manner of a small Gibraltar, Gheria proved to be much less of an obstacle than feared. Its rocky fastness was successfully bombarded beginning on February 11, causing Angria to flee to the nearby encampment of the sympathetic Marathas, effectively abandoning the fort and its petrified inhabitants (mostly women and children) to their fate. Clive and a force of some fifteen hundred men were landed two days later, and Gheria quickly surrendered—"a very easy conquest," wrote Clive to his father—with few casualties suffered on either side. Prizes and plunder were taken as usual and divided among the victors, with Clive enriching his personal coffers by some £5,000.[2]

In the larger scheme of company affairs in India, however, Gheria was a sideshow, although as the governor of Fort William, Roger Drake, nevertheless wrote in a letter to Clive, "I congratulate you on the success against Angria from which the Company may in time reap some benefit. . . . I most heartily wish that some methods may be found out to lessen the exorbitant power of France in India or otherwise our Company will suffer extremely."[3] Clive was of a similar mind. Once Angria's power to harass the East Indiamen had been broken, he was eager to move on to Fort St. David and take up his appointment from which such "methods" might be pursued. Accordingly, he and Margaret sailed from Bombay at the end of April and arrived at the new post on May 14. A quick trip to Madras was made in order for Clive to be admitted formally to the council, and then on June 22, 1756, he returned to Fort St. David to be welcomed as deputy-governor. Clive was now in charge. For the next year and a day, his life would be as full and as militarily exciting as it ever was to be, culminating on June 23, 1757, with the Battle of Plassey, the key encounter that led to the company's domination of Bengal and, by extension, of India itself.

In April 1756, not long before Clive arrived at Fort St. David, the Nawab of Bengal had died. The death of Ali Vardi Khan was propitious, because with the nawab's passing the heretofore rather stable and prosperous province of Bengal was thrown into severe political and commercial ferment. As *subadar*, or "viceroy," of Bengal, Khan had ruled over a vast and wealthy region. His overlordship was not absolute, of course, his power flowing ultimately from that of the Mughal emperor, at that time Farrukhsiyar, in Delhi. But in most practical ways Khan was sovereign, even if the East India Company liked to remind him that its right to trade in Bengal stretched back to 1717 when it had been granted a *farman*, or "charter," to do so by the emperor himself.

Ali Vardi Khan was succeeded by his grandson, Siraj-ud-Daulah, a young man of twenty-three, who had been made crown prince a few years earlier in a controversial move that caused division within both the royal family and the *durbar*, or the royal court. Until not long before his princely elevation Siraj was reputed to be a rather reckless and dissolute youth, but his grandfather's confirmation of him as the successor to the nawabship prompted a significant reformation in his personal behavior. Regardless, in coming to the throne in the spring of 1756, Siraj inherited a tense and shifting situation both within the royal dynasty and in Bengal at large, especially as it concerned the presence of the English there.

Between 1752, when he was made crown prince, and the death of Ali Vardi Khan, Siraj had studied closely the prevailing political and economic situation in Bengal. Unsurprisingly, he shared his grandfather's trepidation at the increasing power and, in his view, arrogance of the Europeans. In particular, he believed the English to be the most bent on expansion and potential usurpation, something that the dying nawab himself had warned of and a state of mind clearly inherited by Siraj. To this end, the new nawab decided to act swiftly and provocatively against the English not long after assuming the throne. Near to his own capital of Murshidabad, located about a hundred miles north of Calcutta along the Hughli River, was the small company factory of Cossimbazar. Unlike Calcutta, which was strongly fortified, Cossimbazar was an easy target for a military adventure, and in June Siraj ordered it taken, which his commanders then proceeded to do rather easily. The nawab's move in this regard was something of a shot across the bow, however, rather than a real offensive step, and it was treated as such by the English. But when Siraj—emboldened by what he took to be apparent company weakness—decided to continue his march south to Calcutta, a generation's worth of Anglo-Mughal tension in Bengal exploded into war.

Early in June 1756 Siraj's troops duly began to move on Calcutta. In defense of Fort William, which lay at its heart, and of Calcutta's suburbs of White Town and Black Town, was a force of about five hundred Europeans—British, Portuguese, and Armenian—and perhaps twice that many sepoys. Governor Drake deployed them in various strategic locations, but their task was virtually impossible against an enemy numbering in the thousands. By June 18, after a relentless and ugly siege, Drake was at wits' end. Two days later, after he put hundreds of women and children on board ships and sent them downriver, Calcutta fell to the nawab. Siraj-ud-Daulah had scored a significant victory over the company and its position in Bengal and perhaps beyond. If it were going to be saved, then decisive action would have to be taken.[4]

While these momentous events were occurring, Clive had been taking up the governorship of Fort St. David. News of the fall of Calcutta did not reach southern India until August, but when it did the tidings of defeat were doubly distressing because in addition to the seizure of Fort William and the destruction of the city, an alleged atrocity had taken place: the incarceration epic that came to be known as the Black Hole of Calcutta. In popular memory, the Black Hole incident survives

**45 Berkeley Square, London**
Clive's townhouse in fashionable Mayfair, the site of his likely suicide.
*Photo by author*

**Clive Steps, Whitehall**
Clive, portrayed grandly as an empire-builder. *Photo by author*

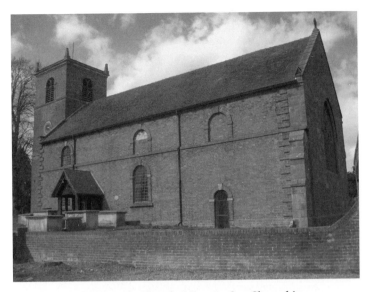

**St. Margaret's Church, Moreton Say, Shropshire**
The simple parish church that Clive called home, with a small plaque to
his memory affixed to the right of the porch. *Photo by author*

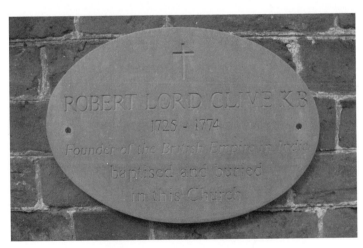

ROBERT LORD CLIVE K.B
1725 - 1774
Founder of the British Empire in India
baptised and buried
in this Church

**St. Margaret's Church, Moreton Say**
Clive's memorial plaque. *Photo by author*

**Styche Hall, near Moreton Say**
The former seat of the Clive family (currently under refurbishment).
*Photo by author*

**Old Grammar School, Market Drayton, Shropshire**
Clive was a (reluctant) student here as a boy. *Photo by author*

**Walcott Hall, near Lydbury North, Shropshire**
The favorite of Clive's various country estates, the façade of which
remains essentially unchanged from his day. *Photo by author*

**Elephant adornment, Walcott Hall**
A nod to Clive's career in India. *Photo by author*

***Robert Clive and Mir Jafar after the Battle of Plassey, 1757***
A romanticized rendition of the moment at which Clive's victory
was sealed. By Francis Hayman, reproduced by permission from
National Portrait Gallery, London

***Stringer Lawrence***
"Father of the Indian Army" and Clive's champion.
By Thomas Gainsborough, c. 1774–1775, reproduced by permission
from National Portrait Gallery, London

in our own day in a way that, short of the 1857 Sepoy Mutiny, nothing else does concerning the history of the British in India. As evidence of the believed oriental penchant for cruelty, the Black Hole occupies a special place in the collective British consciousness, although as Linda Colley has suggested recently, its whelming outrage was not contemporaneous but rather belonged to the more easily censorious Victorians of a century later.[5] She may be right on this point, but clearly to those close to the events in India the outrage was pronounced. As Clive, who described the fall of Calcutta as a "general calamity," wrote to the London directors of the company in October, on the eve of his departure for Calcutta, "every breast here seems filled with Grief, Horror & Resentment; indeed it is too sad a tale to unfold. . . . I flatter myself that this expedition will not end with the taking of Calcutta & that the Company's estate in those parts will be settled in a better & more lasting condition than ever."[6]

Whatever the historiographical complexion put on the Black Hole, there is no doubting its veracity as an event, although there is legitimate debate as to the number of victims involved. Nonetheless, on this point at least its contemporary chronicler, John Zephaniah Holwell, was sure. He was sure, he said simply, because he was one of the 23 survivors out of the 146 defenders of Fort William who had been brutally imprisoned by the victors on the night of June 20. Thrown into a tiny, dank dungeon with only two small windows for air and light, 123 men perished from dehydration and suffocation in a hellish finale to Siraj's victory, he claimed. Given the size of the room in which this horror took place, Holwell most likely exaggerated the number of men involved, perhaps by as much as three or four times, in order to exact a measure of revenge against his captors and to point out his own heroism in having survived the ordeal. Regardless, even if the actual number were considerably smaller, incarceration in this manner on a sweltering Indian night was indeed exceedingly cruel and was viewed rightly by the British as a highly dishonorable act. And that is exactly the way news of it was received in Fort St. David and Madras on August 16.

The British response to Calcutta's fall and the final outrage of the Black Hole that accompanied it was immediate: Clive was recalled to Madras for a meeting of the council and its inner select committee during which time a plan to mount a relief mission in order to retake Calcutta and dislodge Siraj from his unjust perch, or worse, was agreed. The plan and its command structure took almost two months to work out—a process made more complex by the fact that war against the French had recently broken out in North America, with implications for India—but finally, on October 16, the British sailed north.

Clive was in command. "A few weeks ago," he wrote to Roger Drake, just before embarkation, "I was happily seated at St. David's pleased with the thoughts of obtaining your confidence and esteem by my application to the civil branch of the Company's affairs & of improving & increasing the investment, but the fatal blow given to the Company's estate at Bengal has superseded all other considerations."[7] But now everything had changed. "Providence, who is the disposer of all events," wrote Clive in an expression of the rudimentary deism of his time, had intervened and put him in charge of a force of about fifteen hundred men, six hundred of which were Europeans and the rest sepoys.[8] Despite the no-doubt powerful emotion of revenge that the sailing occasioned, the expressed primary aim of the expedition was to recover the company's lost commercial position in Bengal. Clive and his men were the armed wing of the East India Company, intent on brandishing the sword but mindful that it "should go hand in hand with the pen."[9] Those who journeyed north to Calcutta on that day, about four months after its fall, departed also with the entirely natural hope of personal gain. The "prize"—however defined, and whether on land or at sea—was perhaps the leading animator of military conquest in this period. And Clive, like his peers, was keen to reap the expected benefits of smashing Siraj and reasserting the company's claims, guaranteed as they were by the forty-year-old *farman*. "This expedition if attended with success," wrote a highly optimistic Clive to his father on the eve of sailing, "may enable me to do great things."[10]

Personal enrichment would be one of those "great things," as we shall see, but beyond the potential for significant wealth was the possibility of expanded political power, both locally and back in England. At this juncture in Clive's career he had not yet expressed any larger ambitions, either for himself or for his country, beyond those inherent in what already existed for the company in India. But neither his earlier campaigning in the Carnatic nor his recent vanquishing of pirates compared properly to what he was about to undertake at Calcutta. What it might portend for all of Bengal was unknown of course, but in setting out to bend Siraj to his will and to that of the company, Clive was coming close to the fulcrum of his military career in India.

The five-ship British fleet that carried Clive and his men was under the command of Admiral Watson. Progress up the east coast of India was "tedious & difficult," however, with one ship proving "leaky" and another temporarily becoming lost.[11] Hampered by bad weather too, the Ganges Delta where the Hughli River emptied was not reached therefore until early December. Another two weeks were required to sail fifty miles up the Hughli to the dilapidated village of Fulta, which, since the capture of Calcutta, had been turned into a kind of riverine refugee camp for those who had escaped Siraj's attack that summer. Onboard the *Kent*, Clive and the other Council of War members, presided over by Watson, met on December 28 to discuss appropriate next moves. By this point Clive was eager to attack the nawab and took the opportunity of this tension-wracked council meeting to press the point home.[12] In the event, Clive's position won the day. And after a small struggle at the village of Baj Baj, located about halfway to Calcutta, just prior to the New Year, the British approached the city and then took it, surprisingly without much resistance, on January 2, 1757.

The taking of Calcutta and, after a six-month interregnum, putting it back under company authority, was hampered not so much by the resistance of Siraj-ud-Daulah's men, who had mostly fallen back, but rather by intercommand rivalries. Clive, Watson, and Capt. Eyre Coote, a regular army officer who had taken temporary command of the recaptured Fort William, almost fell out over whose charge would be paramount there. After an almost nonsensical struggle, it was agreed that Watson would receive the fort from Clive, who in turn would hand it over to the company. The odd man out in this semifarce was Coote, whose later animus toward Clive, as we shall see, stems from this initial contretemps over Calcutta.

In any event, the English were back in control of the city, but by no means was the situation stable. Watson's squadron was in place, as was Clive's army, but the nawab had a force of anywhere from fifteen thousand to twenty thousand men (although their loyalty would prove dubious) who knew the country well. Complicating the situation for Clive and the company, as always, was the presence of the French. A negotiated "neutrality with the French in the Ganges," wrote Clive in late January, was the preferred course of action, but their factory at Chandernagore, about twenty miles upriver from Calcutta, with its approximately three hundred European troops, loomed as a formidable obstacle.[13] "The French we hear are very busy in fortifying Charnagore," reported Clive to the Select Committee, and if they chose to intervene in the struggle between the nawab and the English there would be trouble.[14] Moreover, the English themselves were unsettled over what to do next. Indeed, Clive, confirmed now as a sometime depressant, regretted "that ever I undertook this expedition."[15] But such despondency was quickly forced aside later in January when the nawab's village of Hughli was attacked with vigour—"early this morning storm'd the Fort," wrote Capt. James Killpatrick to Clive on January 11, "and were in full possession of it by three a clock."[16] The victors went on to plunder its stocks of food and to destroy its fortress walls and buildings. This activity was a prelude to more fighting, but it also put intense pressure on the nawab to negotiate with the company, determined as it was to make him comply with its demands.

To this end Clive enlarged his political activities, consulting widely among local worthies, in an attempt to enlist their help in convincing the nawab to come to terms with the company. "I have but one interest," Clive assured the members of the Select Committee, "which is that of the Company's and as long as that is kept in view I do assure you Gentlemen you shall always find me ready to follow your instructions."[17] The most important of these overtures on behalf of the company was made to the leading banking family in Bengal, the Seths, whose vast financial empire was based in the nawab's capital of Murshidabad. As far as the intra-European struggle was concerned, their sympathies lay with the English. But more than that was the Seths' purported growing dislike of the nawab's rule, a rule that some years before they nonetheless had helped put in place. Clive's penchant for political action became clear in these days of diplomacy and propaganda, but behind the apparent desire for a negotiated settlement with the nawab were the heavy guns of Watson's squadron, the power of which had been already witnessed by all during Hughli's recent destruction.

Meanwhile, despite issuing signals that he really did wish to settle, the nawab also made some provocative military moves that had the understandable effect of making Clive highly distrustful of his words: "I cannot yet," he wrote in frustration to the Select Committee, "judge how sincere he is in his intention towards a peace."[18] After another failed attempt at diplomacy at the end of January, Clive therefore decided to launch a preemptive attack on the nawab's army, encamped as it now was just outside Calcutta, on the other side of the massive earthworks known as the Maratha Ditch. The attack, which began as a modest success thanks largely to the element of surprise and to the fortuitous presence of an early-morning fog bank, turned into a near-disaster, however, as the mist lifted and Clive's force of some two thousand men found themselves broadly exposed to the nawab's fast-riding cavalry and belching cannon. In the event, Clive had to call for a retreat, citing the engagement later as the "warmest service" in which he had ever fought.[19]

There is little doubt that Clive was sobered by this aborted fight; but so too was Siraj. Despite having to retreat, the English and their firepower had carried off more than a thousand of Siraj's men, and in the days that followed, a rather windy Clive made it clear to him that such was a mere foretaste of what the nawab might expect from a full-scale engagement with the technologically superior English. Clive's sabre-rattling had the desired effect because only days later, on February 9, a treaty was signed restoring to the company the position that it had held prior to the outbreak of hostilities the previous year, as well as reparations provided to satisfy the howling complaints of Calcutta's company "gentlemen," and a handful of new privileges. For the moment at least, quiescence reigned in Bengal.

The Treaty of Calcutta briefly put the nawab's machinations from front of mind for Clive. But in their place moved those of the French, whose renewed standing as an official belligerent against the English— which would last until 1763—made their regional presence a constant irritant, as well as a potential ally of Siraj should he choose to throw in his lot with them. Accordingly, Clive and others on the Select

Committee immediately began to think of how the French could be permanently neutralized, thus giving Siraj no recourse but his own troops to bring against the English should the treaty prove to be elastic. After a failed attempt was made at a treaty of neutrality with the French, it was agreed that Clive should march on Chandernagore and that it should be destroyed. Still hoping to negotiate with the French, however, once in range Clive sent word to Chandernagore's president, Peter Renault, that "I have no intention of acting offensively against your nation at present," adding pithily, "whenever I have you may be assured I shall frankly acquaint you with it."[20]

A few days later, on March 13, a demand for the French to surrender was made.[21] Renault refused, however, and the next day Clive and his army of some twenty-five hundred men attacked. The French endeavored to hold their main local settlement with about an equal number of troops, but by March 15 Clive's men had driven the French defenders inside the fort at the center of the devastated town. Clive's soldiers kept them pinned down there for the week that followed until Watson got his ships upriver from which he pounded the fort into submission. The French duly surrendered on March 23, an act that rendered in tatters their position in Bengal, a degraded status from which they would never recover. And, to be sure, it also opened the way for Clive and the English to force the nawab ever more determinedly to do their bidding.

The taking of Chandernagore followed by the destruction of its fort marked a tipping point in Clive's military career in Bengal.[22] The nawab now found himself in a very precarious position, unable to count on any external European help to stave off the English—should they choose to disregard the treaty—and perhaps vulnerable from some within his own camp. Clive used the next few months to enforce upon the nawab the view that the company's true ambition was mercantile in nature and that the armed force that was sometimes used in pursuit of this aim went no further than the protection of trade; that is to say, the company had no interest in becoming Bengal's landlord at the expense of the nawab's territories. Was Clive being honest here? It is hard to know with certitude. In a jubilant letter he had written to his father after the treaty made with Siraj in February, he had expressed the aspiration of becoming "Governor-General of India."[23] We might well forgive Clive's bravado here, if only because no such position then existed and his thinking was really to bind together the three presidencies of Madras, Bombay, and Calcutta, so as to administratively streamline the company's operations in the same way that the French had done successfully at Pondicherry.

In any event, the run of affairs now took a decisive turn against the nawab because the Seths banking family had finally seen enough of his blundering and, fearing for their financial well-being (after all, their wealth came overwhelmingly from trade with the Europeans, especially the English), decided to unleash a scheme by which he might be toppled and the English company made ascendant in Bengal. Clive, with his martial instincts and a well-honed ability to turn a profit, was certainly the right man on the spot to be their enabler, but it must be said that this final act in making Bengal foundational to the British Empire in India came from Indians themselves, the Hindu Seths of Murshidabad, a family of collaborators who fit nicely the later classic interpretation given to such actors on the imperial periphery by Ronald Robinson and Jack Gallagher.[24]

As the Seths' scheming heated up, Clive, not a natural Machiavellian, endeavored to convince the nawab to act more hurriedly on the terms of the February treaty and to place his trust in him. Clive's overtures were not insincere in this regard, but the channels of communication became unsurprisingly muddled, and instead of concord being the result discord ensued. Meanwhile, the key figure in the scheme to displace the nawab, Mir Jafar, had been confirmed. Long a supporter of the nawab, vital to his army's functioning, and a leading aristocrat, Jafar had recently begun to fall out with an increasingly paranoid Siraj. Like the Seths, Mir Jafar feared that the nawab was rapidly endangering the status quo in Bengal, and in order for the highly profitable trading relationship with the English to continue he must be replaced. As it happened, Mir Jafar himself was the nominee of the planners of this putative "revolution."

Clive, having at last given up on Siraj, now began to move in train with the Select Committee's plans, including its drafting of the terms by which Mir Jafar would become the new nawab. Jafar was amenable to whatever the committee had in mind, answering their request for his list of desired terms simply with a blank sheet of paper embossed with his seal.[25] Events now began to unfold quickly, including what came to be the moment by which Clive's (political) morality has been judged most severely by posterity. An indispensable and long-standing Sikh merchant at Calcutta, Omichand (or Amir Chand, as his name is sometimes rendered), friend of the English and just as keen as they were to be rid of Siraj, demanded personal recompense for his facilitator role in the wooing of Mir Jafar. The demand seemed to be accompanied by a veiled threat to reveal the planned coup to the nawab; at least Clive believed that Omichand was committed to such treachery if his demand for at least 5 percent of Siraj's vast wealth was not met. In response, Clive proposed that two sets of terms be drawn up, one to be regarded as real by the committee and Jafar, while the other would be fictitious and designed to convince Omichand that his demands indeed had been met. Clearly, the dark arts of politics were being practiced here, although they were done in response to Omichand's own blackmail. Reciprocal duplicity was baldly at work, not one of Anglo-Indian diplomacy's finest hours, but hardly unique in its long and convoluted history.

In any event, the proposed coup was now afoot, and on June 5 Mir Jafar swore to uphold the terms of the real treaty. A week later, Clive departed Chandernagore, heading northward toward Siraj's army and capital. The time had come to enact the coup. Diplomacy had had its moment, now would come the sword: "I am therefore come this way," wrote Clive, "to see the Articles fulfilled."[26] Clive and Siraj were on course for their climactic meeting, which they would have shortly at the hitherto nondescript village of Plassey.

In going north Clive had with him an army of some three thousand combatants, about two-thirds of whom were sepoys. The balance of his force was European, comprising infantry and artillery, the latter in charge of ten heavy guns. Clive and his European troops boarded boats to journey upriver while next to them along the road that hugged the west bank of the Hughli marched the sepoys. The heat and humidity of Bengal at this time of year were overwhelming, but there was nothing to be done about it, and the troops—especially the marching sepoys—endured it without much complaint, as they almost always did.

A prelude to the main action to come occurred at the fortified village of Cuttwa when Clive sent Eyre Coote ahead of the army to take it in order to capture its ample supplies of food, as well as to announce to Siraj his soon-arrival in the area. Coote and a small body of men did so swiftly, arriving at Cuttwa on June 18, as he reported to Clive, and taking the fort "by storm" before settling into its occupation "with as little plundering as could be expected, as I can venter to say that there is not one European that has took anything." Clive was a stickler for campaign discipline and Coote certainly did not want his triumphant men to run wild, for which he would be blamed. In the same hurriedly scribbled note to Clive, he added, "My greatest satisfaction is to have your approbation."[27] Coote is rather obsequious here, of course, likely a nod to smoothing over their earlier acrimony. Discord between them would return in the not-too-distant future, however, but for the time being both men were resolute in their determination to work together to end the nawab's rule.

No sooner had Clive and the bulk of his army arrived at the still-smoking Cuttwa then a torrential downpour began, evidence of the arrival of monsoon season, driving the men to abandon their sodden tents and take refuge in what was left of the fort and the town's houses and buildings. The ground soon turned to muck, not good for a campaigning army; indeed, the prospect of Clive's army literally becoming bogged down in the floodplains of Bengal was real. Moreover, despite Clive's temporary redoubt at Cuttwa, he was in a rather exposed position, well north of Calcutta and still some forty miles from Murshidabad. Like six years earlier at Arcot, he was now at a decisive moment, and like then he was not at all sure about what should come next, even reporting to the Select Committee that he was "really at a loss" as to what to do: "I beg you will let me have your sentiments, how I ought to act at this critical juncture."[28] The most pertinent question at this point for Clive was whether Mir Jafar was truly in train with him and the Select Committee: "I wait only for some encouragement from Meer Jaffeir to proceed."[29] The question now was not merely political but a pressing military one, and on June 21, amid what he termed was "the greatest anxiety at the little intelligence I receive from Meer Jaffeir," Clive called a Council of War during which his putative ally's unclear position was discussed at length.[30] At the conclusion of the meeting, Clive asked "whether in our present situation without assistance & on our own bottom it would be prudent to attack the Nabob, or whether we should wait 'till joined by some Country Power."[31] Displaying due caution, the council defeated the motion. But Clive was now almost beside himself, and remained so until the next afternoon when in response to his own impatient query to Jafar, a reply finally was made: "When you come near," wrote Jafar reassuringly, "I shall then be able to join you."[32] Relying on his word, Clive decided to move north from Cuttwa, in anticipation of meeting both Jafar and, most importantly, the assembled forces of Siraj with whom he traveled, which were now marching south from Murshidabad. The midpoint of these two converging armies would be the small riverside village of Plassey.

Plassey, or Palashi, as it is called today, comes down to contemporary readers in the sepia-tinged way that does so much else from those long-ago days of British India. Like most other turning points in British imperial history—for example, the Battle of the Plains of Abraham in 1759, or Nelson's Trafalgar in 1805—Clive's Plassey in 1757 has been made both to carry too much freight—and too little. In the years that followed the event, Plassey grew in its capacity to define the assertion of British imperial power in the subcontinent, only later, and with this too-capacious interpretation having run its course, being reduced to a small and, for some, ignominious skirmish. In truth, Plassey indeed was nearer in historical impact to its original interpretation, although no modern historian would claim for it the status of a great battle. Still, neither can it be derided as anything close to a mere "transaction," as some mistakenly have said it to be.[33]

As assured of Jafar's backing as he could hope to be and convinced that a fight with Siraj was inevitable, Clive led his force out of Cuttwa and marched it north until reaching Plassey, his stated goal. They arrived there about one o'clock in the morning on June 23.[34] The village was located on the east side of the Hughli, along a sharp bend in the river. Only a mile distant was the nawab's front line, entrenched in advance of the rest of his gigantic force, which had grown now to at least fifty thousand troops.[35] At Plassey, Clive had his small body of men bivouac in a grove of mango trees, which was surrounded and protected by an earth bank and ditch. Between the grove and the river was a substantial building, a hunting lodge known as Plassey House, used occasionally by the nawab, in which Clive established his headquarters. By the wee hours of the 23rd, Clive's men were settled, but fitfully so, a relatively tiny force in the shadow of the nawab's thousands, a David's army against an assembled Goliath.

As the first rays of morning sun appeared, Clive surveyed the scene from the rooftop of Plassey House. Although badly outnumbered, Clive had faced this sort of circumstance before. Indeed, being (badly) outnumbered was usually the case in his experience of war in India. At roughly 16:1 in troop strength, the nawab's army towered over Clive's small band of fighters. But all was not as it appeared to be. Whereas Clive could count on the sure commitment and martial spirit of virtually all his men, Siraj could not say the same about his. In fact, once the impressive banners, the armor-clad elephants, the mounted guns, and the impatient snorting horses of the cavalrymen were overlooked, the only force that the nawab could absolutely count on was the single division under the command of Mir Madan, his sole immutably loyal commander. Siraj's other three commanders, including Mir Jafar, were disloyal and ready to turn on their erstwhile leader, perhaps even to spike their guns. Clive's natural confidence in times of war was buoyed by this apparent fact, although an almost equal amount of suspicion that perhaps Jafar could not ultimately be trusted initially caused him to blanche at the prospect of taking on this massive enemy: "We must make the best fight of it we can during the day," he remarked with trepidation, "and at night sling our muskets over our shoulders and march back to Calcutta."[36]

Dawn on June 23 brought with it the likelihood of an immediate engagement between the two assembled forces. The nawab's massive army—clearly visible now in the middle distance—had divided in two, one part of which had advanced in order to pound Clive's position in a direct frontal attack, the other to form a wide flanking arc. In response, Clive ordered his troops to proceed out of the mango grove and form a forward line. At this point, around eight o'clock in the morning, both sides opened up with ear-splitting gunnery. As it progressed—"they cannonaded us very briskly"—the damage done to Clive's men was more serious than that to the nawab's.[37] At least thirty of the company's men fell, both dead and wounded, a significant number for a small force. On the other side, however, holes had been punched in the nawab's line, weakening his own men's resolve. Nevertheless, the half-hour firefight was inconclusive, and Clive retired his chastened men back to the relative safety of the grove. The day then proceeded in a rather desultory fashion with the nawab's guns firing without much success over the mud bank and into the grove, and Clive's men returning fire through slits in the bank and from their own field pieces.

For the next few hours nothing of much importance happened. Then around noon, the arrival of thundershowers unleashed a torrent of rain soaking all the combatants to the skin, but more significantly turning the powder of the nawab's guns into mush and therefore causing them to fall silent. Critically, Clive's men had covered their own guns with tarpaulins, thus keeping them dry and giving them the option to fire through the rain. Initially thinking that the same problem had befallen their enemy, however, the nawab's cavalry under the command of the faithful Mir Madan spurred itself into action and galloped toward what they assumed would be a line of muzzled company guns. As soon as they came into close range, however, Clive gave the order for his artillery to fire and they unleashed a murderous volley, one shell of which slammed into the leg of Mir Madan, shattering his thigh bone. Bleeding profusely, he was carried behind lines into the tent of the nawab, expiring in front of his desperate leader, who had no one to rely on now except the turncoat Mir Jafar. Whether the nawab knew for certain at this moment that Jafar was in cahoots with Clive is unknown, but on this particular occasion he told the nawab that the day was too far gone to attack and that his troops should be recalled. Led by disloyal commanders, fully two-thirds to three-quarters of the nawab's troops had failed to fight anyway, and now as evening approached the day seemed lost.

From atop Plassey House, Clive observed these first stirrings of the enemy's retirement. His clothes, like those of his men, were soaked through, and so he went inside to change, asking his subordinates to alert him if the enemy made any significant moves. Scarcely had he put on a dry shirt, however, when his second in command, James Killpatrick, began to move forward by leading a detachment of men to occupy the ground in front of the hunting lodge leading up to the larger of two excavated water tanks. The unauthorized and risky move was a good one, however, and Clive quickly called up additional troops to reinforce the new position and to put his own stamp on the promising maneuver. Hot fire was then directed at the nawab's now straggly line, which had the effect of drawing it out that much more. Meanwhile, a simultaneous English barrage prevented the enemy's cannon from being shifted into position owing to panic among the oxen required for the job. Indeed, oxen were not alone in their panic as among the nawab's troops themselves it also set in as officers began to fall and terrified elephants began to rage and stampede, and die, as happened to at least three of the great beasts.[38]

The battle was now beginning to resemble a melee. Clive then seized what would prove to be the final initiative and called forward the last of his troops held in reserve for an all-out assault on the faltering enemy. Charging forward, Clive's troops took the mound on the far side of the large tank, which had been the enemy's key position. The nawab's men now broke and ran, as he had done already, escaping the field on camelback in a mad dash back to Murshidabad. A clutch of thirty or so French troops who had been in the fray also beat a hasty retreat, although continuing to fire as they did so.[39] Timepieces now read about five o'clock in the afternoon. The Battle of Plassey was over. The nawab had lost some five hundred men killed, the English about twenty, plus some thirty sepoys, altogether a "trifling" number to Clive.[40] As battles go, this was no exhibition of great tactical skill, even less was it one of extreme carnage. But Plassey's straightforward execution and relatively few casualties belied its capstone effect on the ascendancy of the East India Company in Bengal. Siraj-ud-Daulah's great army—however badly led and loosely deployed—had been defeated, and Clive and the company stood on the brink of assuming control of the province's equally great wealth.

"The Revolution effected by your own gallant conduct," wrote the members of the Select Committee to Clive from Calcutta on June 29, six days after the battle, "and the bravery of the officers and soldiers under you is of such extraordinary importance not only to the Company but to the British Nation in general that we think it incumbent to return you and your officers our sincere thanks on behalf of his Britannick Majesty & the East India Company for your behaviour, on this critical and important occasion."[41] In Clive's initial accounts of the battle, he had used the term "revolution" to describe what had happened, and it fast became the word of choice in describing Plassey's impact on the company's fortunes in Bengal. Indeed, in the months afterward Clive's language remained similarly hyperbolic, as on the occasion of a letter sent to one of the company directors, William Belchier, in August in which he cited the victory at Plassey as sparking a "grand Revolution brought about in this country by the Forces under my command."[42] Similarly, and in even more ecstatic terms, he wrote to his father saying that "a revolution has been effected (by means of the military only) scarcely to be paralleled in history."[43]

A short time earlier, on June 29, a triumphant Clive had entered Murshidabad accompanied by about five hundred European troops and sepoys, there to be feted by the equally happy Seths and by the recently returned Mir Jafar.[44] The defeated nawab had already slipped out of the city in disguise, only—in something akin to what would be Louis XVI's desperate "Flight to Varennes" in 1791—to be recognized and brought back home to face death. "I have received a note from the Nabob," wrote Clive to the Select Committee on June 30, "informing me that Surajah Dowlah is taken."[45] Siraj's execution, alas, in which Clive played no part, was even more grisly than would be that of the guillotined French king, as he was stabbed to death by members of Mir Jafar's family who then paraded his broken body through the streets of his former capital. "Surajah Dowlah is no more," Clive flatly informed the Select Committee.[46]

Clive's position as military conqueror made his feting go on at length, something with which he was distinctly uncomfortable and sought to end. Having succeeded in doing so, over the next few days he met with Mir Jafar on a couple of occasions, acknowledging him as the rightful and new nawab, and with him beginning to undertake the serious business of determining the actual extent of Siraj's riches before dividing them up among all the stakeholders in the victory at Plassey. Thus it was that the Seths were designated to supervise the apportionment of the lakhs of rupees, the jewels, and the plate that had lately comprised Siraj's vast treasure trove of wealth. A few days later a fleet of more than seventy local craft was enlisted to ferry the precious cargo down the Hughli to Calcutta. "Yesterday," wrote Clive in triumph to the Select Committee, "we began to embark the treasure in boats."[47] In so doing the spoils of war were demonstrated more gaudily than they had ever been before in the company's history in India.

But the bounty was simply an extreme affirmation of the practice of presents and prize-taking that undergirded all military conquest in the eighteenth century. A later generation and, indeed, a subsequent age, would condemn it by using their own different standards, but no one at the time considered it anything other than the just rewards of a seminal victory won. As thousands of rupees and heaps of glittering jewels were dispensed to members of the Select Committee, to army officers, and even—in a much smaller way—to the native residents of Calcutta, Clive's share was ultimately made out to total the enormous sum of £234,000. In modern terms there is no easy way to translate this figure, but one of approximately US$50 million would be reasonably close. This was staggering wealth, to be sure, and its transfer to Clive immediately gave him extraordinary lifetime riches and the means to rise as high in Georgian society as money would allow. Principally, this meant regaining a seat in Parliament and to do so he vowed to his father, in reference to his previous attempt a few years earlier that had ended in disappointment, "If I can get into Parliament I shall be very glad but no more struggles against the Ministry. I choose to be with them."[48] Such aspirations together with his vast newly acquired wealth—"You may now order the Rector to get everything ready for the reparation of old Styche," he added—would also, of course, bring with it attendant challenges to Clive's name and honor, as we shall soon see.

# Wealth and Power

CLIVE'S POSITION IN THE summer of 1757 was clearly strong, although the full extent of it, and that of the company, was not yet apparent. Siraj-ud-Daulah's defeat and subsequent bloody demise had put an exclamation point on the events at Plassey. But some of the old nawab's supporters remained in the field and so fighting continued apace, although none of it involved Clive directly. Rather it was Eyre Coote who pursued the remnant-French who were under the command of Jacques Law, an inglorious job and one for which Coote did not receive the thanks he deserved—neither from the permanently disaffected Clive nor from anyone else. Clive thought himself through with fighting, and as it turned out, he was right. Indeed, after the severe exertions of the previous months, he was planning to soon be free of India altogether, to "steer my course for home," as he put it in a letter to Robert Orme.[1] "I wait for nothing," he informed company director William Belchier in August, "but the settlement of these provinces to begin my voyage for old England." Referring to his campaigning father, who he rightly assumed was making the rounds in London singing his victorious son's praises, Clive enjoined Belchier to try to "end or moderate his expectations, for altho' I intend getting into Parliament & have hopes of being taken some notice of by his Majesty. . . . I know my Father's disposition leads this way which proceeds from his affection for me."[2]

As it turned out, Clive's departure for home would not come for two more years, a result of the extent of the Plassey-induced "revolution of much greater consequence to both publick [*sic*] & private," as Clive expressed it in a letter to the secretary of war, Lord Barrington.[3] In the meantime, his victory at Plassey, its accompanying riches, and his exalted position at the nawab's court, or *durbar*, meant that Clive began to acquire the bearing and train of a noble—at least as far as Bengal was concerned. He was justifiably confident in the historical importance of that summer's events, although he expressed it with a touch of ruefulness to Orme: "I am possessed of volumes of materials for the continuance of your History, in which will appear Fighting, tricks, Chicanery, Intrigues, Politics & the Lord knows what. In short there will be a fine field for you to display your Genius in. . . . I have many particulars to explain to you relating to this said History which must be published." But, as befit his exalted post, he was rich enough to ask for "200 shirts," which were to be "the finest & best you get for love or money" and "a compleat set of table linen . . . and of Chintz furniture."[4] All in all, Clive was settling well into his imperial role in Bengal.

The brace of years in Bengal that followed Plassey was full of the exercise of near-dictatorial power by Clive, not so much because he was given to its assumption, but rather because Mir Jafar, as nawab, was unable to act up fully to the demands and expectations of his position as guarantor of the 1757 treaty settlement. At the outset of the new regime, Clive had been sincere and conscientious in disclaiming a role for himself or for the company in Bengal beyond that of "commerce."[5] But his professed political disinterest did not last long in the face of what Clive believed was Jafar's bumbling and resistance to his own sage advice. Still, throughout Clive maintained a proper respect for the nawab publicly, while privately writing to him of the entwined nature of the English's fate in Bengal, "twisted with yours like two threads."[6] But he was also under no illusions about what it would take to ensure the company's exalted position there. As Clive described it, "peace is the most valuable of all Blessings, but it must be made sword in hand in this Country, if we mean to preserve our present possessions."[7]

The silken bonds of which Clive spoke, however, came to be frayed easily, and during the autumn of 1757 and into 1758 such fraying is exactly what happened. While his health flared up at this time—"I am sorry to hear you are troubled with the Gout," wrote George Clive to his infirm cousin in March, "but," he ended on a rhyming note, "hope you'll soon again be very stout"—Clive's position in relation to the company was enlarged and confirmed when he was named Governor of Bengal in February, ending a brief experiment by the London directors of a gubernatorial rotation.[8] Another significant change took place some months later in August when Warren Hastings, then just twenty-five years of age and destined to be as deeply linked with British India as Clive himself, was appointed company resident at the nawab's *durbar*.

Hastings was a coming man in Clive's Bengal. Effectively orphaned as a child, he had been brought up by a paternal uncle and given an excellent education at Westminster School in London before gaining an appointment with the East India Company. He had arrived in Calcutta in 1750 as a seventeen-year-old writer with hopes similar to those Clive had had six years earlier in Madras, although Hastings was not much inclined to military service. Nonetheless, he later served as a volunteer in Clive's army at Plassey, during which time he made a strongly favorable impression upon the senior man. Clive's recommendation secured Hastings's residency appointment in Murshidabad. "You have behaved to me with so much friendship since you have been appointed to Command," wrote Hastings to Clive later, and once Hastings was in place the two men worked together closely.[9]

For Hastings the two years he served at the nawab's *durbar* were an intense education in the company nexus that was Bengal commerce and politics. Clive, ensconced at Fort William in Calcutta, corresponded with him constantly, attempting to stay on top of all that the nawab was doing (or not doing) and ensuring that the company's name and strength remained exalted within the *durbar*. Whether it was the whereabouts of the conniving Omichand, who had absconded from Calcutta, the restlessness of the nawab's (unpaid) troops, or indeed the deteriorating financial position of the nawab, Clive's missives to Hastings were thorough and regular.[10]

In this way Clive gradually came to the conclusion that as much as Mir Jafar had been a necessary and ultimately cooperative ally in the overthrow of Siraj-ud-Daulah, his continued occupancy of the nawab's throne could come only at the detriment of the company's standing in Bengal. As such, Jafar—as surely as Siraj before him— had to be replaced. Clive's realization in this regard came slowly, and it developed in the midst of his work to consolidate the company's gains against the still-existent rivalries of both the French and the Dutch. But as strong as Clive was locally, his reputation in England had not been transformed by the victory at Plassey and therefore he was no unalloyed politico-military star at home. He still carried with him a grasping reputation, made worse by the irrepressible metropolitan politicking of his father. Moreover, in an age when it was assumed that the best kind of military officer came only from the aristocracy, Clive's provincial background and his early days as "a dirty writer"— as one overwrought MP, William Beckford, expostulated in the Commons—were held against him. Indeed, his triumph at Plassey was not interpreted by most as a great imperial victory at the time news of it reached England in the autumn of 1757, but as more of a local triumph. There were, however, exceptions to this muted interpretation, and for Clive, one of them could not have come from a better source: the Secretary of State for the Southern Department, William Pitt. In December, in Parliament, he heaped praise upon the absent officer. "We had lost our glory, honour and reputation everywhere but in India," Pitt said assuredly, in cataloging the defeats of the recently begun Seven Years' War. "There the country had a heaven-born general who had never learned the art of war, nor was his name enrolled among the great officers. . . . Everyone knows that I mean Colonel Clive."[11]

Pitt would remain Clive's champion in the years to come and soon enough would receive from Clive his clearest-ever statement of the enlarged view of what the company might be able to accomplish in Bengal. In a letter to Pitt written on January 1, 1759, Clive referred to the responsibilities now borne by the company and wondered if it might not be necessary to gain "the Nation's assistance to maintain so wide a dominion." The provision of such assistance would ensure both the company's success and, by extension, that of the country, as "there will be little or no difficulty in obtaining the absolute possession of these rich kingdoms." In effect, Clive assured Pitt, "so large a Sovereignty" was the natural course for British affairs to take in Bengal, "an acquisition, which . . . would prove a source of immense wealth to the Kingdom." Reinforcing the suggestion, Clive argued that a forward stance in India would foil the European competition and staunch the drain on the public purse that "has been too much the case with our possessions in America." Ending on a confident military note, Clive pointed out that altogether these ends could be achieved with merely "a small force from home," supplemented by "any number of Black Troops, who, being both much better paid and treated by us than by the Country Powers, will very readily enter into our Service."[12]

And there Clive left it, a blueprint for the sustained exertion of British power in India. As we shall see, Pitt was to look with great favor on these plans.[13] Meanwhile, in India, Clive was now surer than ever that a change in the position of nawab must be made if such plans were to be realized. Before that would happen, however, Clive was the recipient of a significant gift, the sort accorded to one of his rank as commander of a Moghul district. Called a *jagir*, it rendered to the holder the annual revenues of a given district, and as it turned out for Clive, his district was the one that surrounded Calcutta—the amount of which totaled some 300,000 rupees, or approximately £27,000. The jagir was handed to Clive personally by Mir Jafar in June 1759, written in Persian on a parchment scroll, or a *perwannah*, contained within a maroon-colored silk bag, which is how it remains today, stored in a box at the National Library of Wales.[14]

Clive's jagir, alas, would prove to be an Achilles' heel to him, forever dogging his reputation as a too-eager recipient of Bengali wealth. In Clive's later battles, both with the company and in Parliament, the jagir would be a point of harsh dispute. At the time of its presentation, however, it was seen as another rightfully granted form of recompense for services rendered; although its effect was to put Clive in the anomalous position of being both a company servant and a Mughal commander, and thereby a collector of company rent.

As 1759 wore on Clive had to deal also with the constant pinprick imprecations of the Dutch from their base at Cinsura, north of Calcutta. They were finally put down in November, without Clive himself being required to fire a shot. Once he could at last be sure that neither the Dutch nor the French posed a threat to the hard-won English ascendancy in Bengal, his thoughts again turned resolutely toward home. In Calcutta among the relatively small European community, however, there was much trepidation at the prospect of Clive's impending departure. On December 5, eighty-seven of their number wrote a heartfelt letter to Clive begging him to stay in this "very unsettled" country. Referencing the earlier fall of Calcutta as the "miserable catastrophe of June 1756," they enjoined him to "remain among us, untill [sic] such time as the posture of affairs shall wear a more favourable aspect."[15] Appreciative as he was of this sentiment, Clive was not about to postpone an already delayed departure for England, however. Margaret Clive too was keen to sail for home, and when they did so, on February 21, 1760, there was much relief mixed with anticipation of the life that awaited them in England.

In leaving Bengal when he did, Clive did not bequeath to it the kind of stability and prosperity that the victory at Plassey had portended. The once-burgeoning treasury was now nearly depleted owing to the large military expenses incurred over the previous three years. Equally as pressing, the incompetent Mir Jafar remained as nawab, Clive having not yet engineered the removal of this, as he judged him now, "very great fool."[16] The job of doing so, therefore, would fall to his successor, Henry Vansittart, a friend of Clive's from their shared early days as writers, the former at Fort St. David and Clive, of course, at Fort St. George. His appointment as governor to succeed Clive was made in November 1759, but Vansittart did not arrive in Calcutta to take up the post until July of the following year. In the meantime, John Zephaniah Holwell of Black Hole fame assumed the position of acting governor and, while doing so, contemplated removing Mir Jafar as nawab immediately and replacing him with his more compliant son-in-law, Mir Kasim.[17] Once arrived, Vansittart completed the plan, with assistance from Warren Hastings, and Jafar was overthrown in October 1760 in a bloodless coup. If Clive began the "revolution" in Bengal at Plassey, then here was evidence of its continuing logic. But for the Clives all of that was very far from view as they arrived in England on July 9, 1760, after a very fast voyage home on the speedy bark, *Royal George*.

Clive and his wife had been away from England for more than five years. Their son, Ned, who had just learned to walk when they had last seen him, had grown into a talkative six-year-old.[18] Clive's proud parents were there once again to greet them in London. Rebecca Clive had written to them earlier in Bengal about the Plassey victory being a "great and glorious success. My joy upon the occasion is more then I can express," and she was ecstatic at their return, the early part of which was spent living in the parental house located in the City on St. Swithins Lane.[19] Only a few days after their arrival, Clive had an audience of the aging King George II, who, like Clive, had led troops into battle; indeed, he was the last British monarch ever to do so having fought at Dettingen in 1743. But only a few months after meeting Clive, in October 1760, the king died and was succeeded by his eldest son who became George III. The East India Company directors were very warm in their welcome home of him too. Clive was a hero, although he was not celebrated in the way that General Wolfe, who had fallen recently at Quebec, had been.

Clive was rich and he was ambitious, ready to make the most of what these two attributes might mean in the complex aristocratic world of Georgian Britain. To live like a nobleman of course would cost a great deal of money, and that he had in abundance, largely owing to the annual remuneration provided by the jagir. Houses were either rented or purchased in short order. For someone in his (aspiring) social station that meant a London town house, as well as one in the country. To that end, early in 1761 he rented 45 Berkeley Square, which would be purchased subsequently for £10,500. A very smart West End town house, it belonged to Lord Ancram and was located near everything of importance in London, both political and fashionable. The property's Palladian façade spoke of status and wealth, which looks much today as it did in Clive's lifetime. Almost concurrently, in March 1761 he "purchased Lord Montfort's estate for £70,000."[20] Located in south Shropshire, it consisted of 7,500 acres and was intended to become a new family seat. In the meantime, a house in the country was rented, Condover, near Shrewsbury.

Clive was also not reluctant to spread his wealth around. His parents benefited from an immediate reconstruction of the old Styche house in Shropshire. It, too, still stands, having lately become a rather grand block of flats situated in a verdant garden and surrounded by undulating farmland. Clive's sisters each received an annual sum— "kindness to my girls," as his mother put it—and his former stellar colleague in battle, Stringer Lawrence, an annuity.[21] For his part, the otherwise voluble Lawrence was rendered almost "speechless" by this act of generosity, writing to Clive that he was "at a loss to find words sufficiently to thank you."[22]

At this point in his life Clive had no intention of returning to India. His aspirations now lay in England, in the acquisition of real estate and in the consolidation of his wealth and putative position in society. Naturally, this meant that he must spend a considerable amount of time in London, but the great metropolis was never his favorite place. Born and bred in the country, he was always at his best there and over the next few years demonstrated his attachment to it constantly, especially to his native Shropshire. These years were also troubled by ill-health. Clive referred to his malady as "rheumatysm," a contemporary catchall used to describe joint-pain, gout, or chronic intestinal upset. Whatever the nature of the inexact diagnosis that he would always be given, it remained "the most terrible disorder" to him.[23] In the manner of the day rest and water cures were prescribed, both of which could be best had at the spa town of Bath, and so it was there that he went and stayed for long periods.

He had already begun to do so when, in the spring of 1761, he was elected to Parliament for Shrewsbury, an eventuality that Richard Clive had been working on since his own election as MP for Montgomery—a pocket or "rotten" borough controlled by the Earl of Powis—two years earlier. Clive's election was unopposed, and therefore unlike his first parliamentary experience in 1754–1755, he took up his seat with no worry of contestation. Clive also allied himself—as earlier he had told his father he would do—with the ministry, but did so in a manner that was briefly unsettling. And so while Clive chose therefore to lend to the Duke of Newcastle his support, Prime Minister William Pitt, his erstwhile champion, had come to support one of King George III's ministerial nominees, the Earl of Bute. This bit of political jockeying was sticky for Clive, and indeed Bute did succeed Newcastle as the king's chief minister in 1762. Despite Pitt's past support, however, Clive as an inexperienced MP chose to stay close to the wizened

Newcastle and as a reward was recommended by him for the peerage that he had continued to hope his triumph at Plassey would yield.

Accordingly, Clive received his peerage as Baron Clive of Plassey in March 1762 in the waning days of Newcastle's government. The barony was Irish rather than British, a small disappointment to him because of its lower prestige, but the social imprimatur was clear nonetheless, putting a capstone on his magnificent wealth that now was likely in the vicinity of £300,000. Such affluence brought with it, of course, jealousies and opposition, which would grow and indeed hound Clive for the rest of his life. But in 1761–1762 it was the jagir alone that became the cause of deep animosity toward him by some, and the source of a protracted struggle within the East India Company itself. On one side of the conflict was Clive; on the other was Laurence Sulivan, at that time chairman of the company's Court of Directors and otherwise a figure of authority at the Leadenhall Street headquarters for most of the period between 1755 and his death in 1786. Sulivan had gone out to Bombay in the 1730s as a private merchant, joining the company in 1741. The two men met in India, but a sustained encounter did not occur until both had returned to England in 1753. After that, while initially remaining on cordial terms, the dyspeptic Sulivan and the prickly Clive grew in mutual animosity before falling out completely over the government's proposed terms for the treaty that would settle the outcome of the Seven Years' War in 1763. Sulivan's approach to the treaty, which proposed a restoration to France of at least some of the Indian territories lost earlier by Dupleix, was heartily opposed by Clive. At the same time Sulivan intimated to Clive that the continued holding of his jagir might not stand in light of growing opposition to it within the company. After all, why should Clive and not the company itself be the recipient of the nawab's favor in this regard, especially when its financial position in Bengal was suffering?

Once the justice of Clive's jagir entered the picture the company became irreparably factionalized, with Clive lining up supporters to oppose the equally backed Sulivan. For Clive, this challenge both to his wealth and, by extension, to his honor, was a call to battle, and he vowed to "hurt" Sulivan "if he attempts to hurt me."[24] Their keen animosity was heightened in 1762–1763 by the deepening of the fiscal crisis in Bengal under the ill-starred governorship of Henry Vansittart.

Despite his best efforts, Vansittart was not able to right the listing financial ship of the company in its relations with the new nawab, Mir Kasim. In Kasim, Vansittart and the company got more than they had bargained for in engineering the deposition of the old nawab. Kasim was determined to reassert the nawab's privileges, which had eroded under the increasingly dreamy Mir Jafar—who had been accused, among other things, of spending too much time with his hemp pipe. As such, he began to challenge the company's trading privileges, which, though certain of them were guaranteed by both the original imperial *farman* and by the 1757 treaty, were being exceeded by English and European traders who disliked having their private access to trade goods and their profit margins encroached upon by native traders and merchants alike.

In this regard the situation in Bengal was becoming increasingly explosive. At home, the company's internecine wrangling continued apace also with many months of political tension capped by the scheduled periodic election of directors in April 1763. In the event, the election was a litmus test of who supported whom between Clive and Sulivan, with the latter man ultimately winning the day. The result was that shortly after the election Sulivan as chairman sent an order to Vansittart in Calcutta to stop all payments of Clive's jagir. Clearly, this action was the "hurt" that Clive had spoken of earlier in his contest with Sulivan, and with his martial blood up he too wrote Vansittart threatening a lawsuit against him and the Bengal Council if they should comply with the command of his nemesis. Even more disputatious months ensued in London therefore, while at the same time conditions deteriorated for the company in India. "Poor Bengal," as Clive had written earlier, and not without some hubris, "hath been in one scene of confusion ever since I left it & very little money collected."[25]

Confusion in Bengal soon enough turned to violence. In July, Vansittart signed a declaration of war brought on by the previous month's attack by Mir Kasim's men on the company's factory at Patna. Almost fifty Europeans were slaughtered in the surprise attack, and in response Vansittart and the council summarily removed Kasim as nawab, handing the throne back to the surprised but receptive Mir Jafar. Kasim, naturally, was not about to go quietly, and together with his allies, such as the Nawab of Oudh, he launched a full-scale offensive against the company. For more than a year this escalating war would drag on, the reports of it that got back to England heightening the already archanxiety over the state of affairs in Bengal and therefore of the company's future.

Clive was privy to these reports, and they contributed significantly to his ongoing disquiet over the future of his embattled jagir. They also, of course, contributed to a wider fall in confidence in the company by investors in the city of London, with its stock tumbling in value accordingly. To protect his own position at least, Clive entered into a political deal with the new prime minister, George Grenville. In exchange for his unqualified support of the ministry, Clive asked that the government exert pressure on the Court of Directors to maintain the jagir for the next ten years. Grenville proceeded to do just that, and the decision of the company's parliament, the General Court of Proprietors, in April 1764 confirmed the maintenance of such payments by the underwhelming vote of 514 in favor to 453 against. As the vote showed, the company was effectively split over the question. Still, "I have no doubt," wrote the company reviewer of the case, Charles Yorke, "upon the right of Lord Clive to the rent or Jaghire demanded."[26]

Despite the close vote by the proprietors, Clive's income from the jagir was safe and, as it turned out, would last for the rest of his life. But the controversy at home and, more pointedly, in Bengal spurred both Clive and his supporters to contemplate his return to Calcutta, something that the General Court had endorsed along with the maintenance of Clive's jagir. Another term in India therefore now was in prospect and Clive did not shy away from it, although it can hardly have been an ideal move at this juncture in his life even if there, as he wrote ironically to his father, "I enjoy my health better then in England."[27] If he went back to India it would be to enforce on the company's servants in Bengal new (and unpopular) rules designed to limit or even eliminate the taking of gifts and the extent of private trading, admittedly ironic rules for Clive to transmit given his own history of benefiting from both of these things. But times for the East India Company had changed. The nawab must be placated and the warfare must end if the company's fortunes in Bengal were to be secured.

Not much time elapsed between the vote to endorse the jagir and the promulgation of new rules for the company in Bengal before Clive took his leave of England.[28] But the tumult of the previous year had not, however, prevented him from continuing to consolidate his landed position, most notably with the acquisition of an estate in a highly desirable location in southwest Shropshire near the Welsh border. Walcot Hall cost him the enormous sum of £92,000, but it was exactly the kind of country house with broad acres (some 6,000) that he believed matched his aggrandized position in society, and it—rather than the originally envisioned Montfort estate—became his chief residence for the rest of his life, remaining in the Clive family until well into the twentieth century. Nonetheless, despite Walcot's price, the house itself was in need of renovation, which it began to receive very soon after Clive took possession. Indeed, for most of the time he was in Bengal the house and grounds were worked on by local laborers, who, in stark contrast to the riches available to some in India, received the going rate of just seventeen pence per day.[29] Importantly too, the acquisition of Walcot allowed him to increase his parliamentary interest by having his trustworthy cousin, George Clive, stand successfully for an almost immediate local by-election. Clive's relationship with his cousin was always close and often paternal, as in the time a few years earlier when he had cautioned George about his apparent spendthrift ways, urging him to consider "what economy is necessary, & what your income is likely to be for the rest of your days, for altho' I may hereafter have interest to serve you & [Edmund] Maskelyne . . . yet there is no dependence to be had on the smiles of the Great, & I may be always at variance with them."[30]

Clive sailed for India on June 4, taking along with him, among others, his faithful brother-in-law, Mun Maskelyne. Parting from Margaret naturally was sorrowful, but he hoped the separation would not be for too long: "Let us look forward towards the happy day of our meeting," he wrote from Portsmouth on the day of his departure, "which I think cannot be farther distant than two years." And to reassure her that his life would not be in peril, at least from warfare, Clive added, "The busy scene in which I shall be employed without embarking in any more military undertakings will greatly shorten our time of absence."[31]

Clive, now two years into his barony, had recently been made knight of the Order of the Bath by the new young king, George III. These were preferments to be enjoyed, to be sure, but doing so in England would have to wait. So, also, would his parliamentary position, his properties, and his wife and four children. Bengal beckoned, the price, one supposes, for ensuring the future payments of his jagir and perhaps the survival of the company itself. And so with Margaret "reconciled to my departure in a manner consistent with that good sense which I know you to be mistress of," a grimly determined Clive boarded the East Indiaman the *Kent* and sailed for the third, and what would prove to be his final, time for India.[32]

*6*

# Bengal Again

CLIVE'S VOYAGE OUT TO INDIA covered the usual route, across to Brazil and then down around the Cape and up to the subcontinent. But the passage was inordinately slow, a full four months elapsing before the *Kent*—tacking mainly into steady headwinds—reached Rio de Janeiro on October 7. Clive found the journey tedious, from the on-board company to the diet, and regaining his land-legs in Rio was a welcome change from restlessly pacing the quarterdeck.

In port he caught up on his mail, sending a long letter to Margaret in which he made clear, yet again, his intention to have this sojourn back to India be as brief as possible. "Nothing," he emphasized to her, "shall induce me to stay in Bengal beyond the year 1765."[1] In the meantime, he later assured her concerning the children, "by your strict attention to their education and morals, you will render our family a much more important service than by accompanying your husband."[2] By early in the New Year 1765 Clive had reached Cape Town, writing once more to his wife in the same vein that he was "very impatient to reach India that I may the sooner return to that place where everything is so dear to me."[3] But four months' transit remained until Clive would arrive in Calcutta, which he did on May 3, "to take possession of a Government which I find in a more distracted state, if possible, than

I had reason to expect." "But," he added resolutely to Maj. John Carnac, who was just then away leading the company army in Oudh, "I'm determined not to be embarrassed by the errors of others, if in my power to remedy them."[4]

En route to Calcutta, Clive had stopped at Madras where he was brought up to date on events in India while he had been at sea. The most important of these was that Mir Jafar was dead, Mir Kasim had been defeated, and the company's army under Carnac had begun a march to Delhi. The latter was not something that Clive endorsed, thinking it too grand an undertaking and outside the boundaries of the company's main business in Bengal. But back in London none of this mattered to young Ned, who, when he eventually read about the march the following year, wrote hyperbolically and in obvious admiration of his far-away father: "I heard you were arrived safe at Bengal, and marching up to Delhi, at the head of six thousand men."[5]

Upon arriving in Calcutta, Clive, somewhat more prosaically than imagined by his son, took up residence in Fort William, which, since the "mortifications to the Company," as he had earlier described the events of 1756, had been reconstructed.[6] His own house within the fort indeed was palatial, complete with scores of servants and a body-guard. He immediately began to pour through administrative documents in an effort to acquaint himself with the exact state of the company's affairs in Bengal. He did not like what he found, as it confirmed his suspicions about rampant graft and serial laxity. He labeled his discoveries "shocking" and set his mind to rooting out all the abuses committed by company servants in the service of carrying out a general reform of its Bengali operations.[7]

Beginning with enforcing the company's recently passed rules prohibiting presents, Clive quickly exerted his authority over the Bengal Council, especially over one of its, in his view, recalcitrant members, John Johnstone. From the moment of Clive's arrival Johnstone resisted his attempts to reform the rules and conditions under which the company's servants conducted their business. It escaped no one, of course, that Clive—the recipient of great presents in his early days in India including, most notably, the ongoing largesse of the jagir—was now clamping down on his junior colleagues for doing much of what he had done. And his talk of "corruption" and a prevailing situation that needed to be "cleansed" was, to many, the height of hypocrisy.[8] A healthy sense of occupational survival meant that most of the company's servants in Bengal accepted in silence this (retrospective) inconsistency, but not Johnstone. He challenged Clive at the first meeting held to discuss the requirements of the new regime and was put down swiftly. Despite his peremptory silencing, however, there was much more disquiet to come.

Prior to Clive's arrival in Calcutta, Johnstone had been included in a small party of company men who had taken it upon themselves to install a new nawab to succeed the recently deposed and little-lamented Mir Kasim. Again, doing so was hardly out of the ordinary in the context of recent Bengal history as exemplified by Clive himself, but such king-making and present-taking was not going to be tolerated any longer—at least not by Clive—and so Johnstone and his colleagues were reported to the Court of Directors in London. Johnstone, enraged by this action, chose to resign in disgust but not before he had sent his own letter to the directors in which he denounced Clive's jagir. Naturally, as governor Clive was not about to be the loser in this contretemps, but certainly it was not a good way in which to commence his new term, which as he would explain later to the directors, was to have comprised "a complete plan for the regulating and conducting your important concerns, political, civil, and military, in Bengal."[9] But as upsetting as the Johnstone affair was, its bad taste in Clive's mouth would soon be washed away because his impending masterstroke for both the company and ultimately for Britain would come shortly when he headed upcountry and returned with the imperial *diwani* in hand.

If Clive's victory at Plassey had made the company's military ascendancy in Bengal all but inevitable, then his acquisition for it of the *diwani* (that is, appointment by the Moghul emperor to collect revenue in Bengal, as well as in the neighboring provinces of Bihar and Orissa) was the battle's financial analogue. In late June 1765 Clive set off inland to reach a new settlement with the emperor, Shah Alam II, or the Great Mogull as Clive referred to him, and with the Nawab of Oudh, Shuja-ud-Daulah, Kasim's former ally.[10] This governor's tour would see Clive cover seven hundred miles in the steamy heat of the North Indian plains. Initially, he traveled to Patna and then on to the Hindu holy city of Benares (today's Varanasi) on the banks of the Ganges where he met with Shuja. Clive succeeded in convincing him to continue in agreement with the company's rising position, establishing relations with the British that would last for almost a hundred years until the outbreak of the Sepoy Mutiny in 1857. From there in early August Clive proceeded to Allahabad where he met with the emperor. Even though Shah Alam's power had withered, the tradition of imperial grandeur continued to surround him, most especially that of ceremonial form. Two days of negotiations yielded an agreement by which the emperor would receive the revenues from a pair of erstwhile provinces and an annual payment of tribute from the company. In return, he granted the *diwani* of Bengal, Bihar, and Orissa to the East India Company. The ceremony marking the agreement took place on August 12 in one of Clive's traveling tents, not exactly as depicted in Benjamin West's later famous rendering of the scene, of course, but grand in its way all the same. The clearest foundational period of British India, the eight years between Plassey and the granting of the *diwani*, was now complete.

"I have concluded a peace for the Company which I hope will satisfy and obtained from the King a grant of revenue of two millions sterling," wrote Clive to his father after having returned triumphantly to Calcutta in September.[11] Indeed, the *diwani* was a singular diplomatic victory, and with it the financial guarantee of which Clive had written some years earlier to William Pitt had come to pass, although the estimate given turned out to be too high.[12] In any event, despite this achievement the months that followed were not nearly as rewarding for Clive as they might have been had not his reformist zeal extended more closely into military affairs. But since his remit included the army his reforming eye naturally fastened upon it. Here, perhaps surprisingly, he found the resistance to be even more swift and pronounced than it had been in the financial and administrative area.

As alluded to in the previous chapter, costs incurred by the army had been the preponderant cause of the company's financial straits in Bengal in recent years, and Clive set out to decrease them through the usual means of rationalization and retrenchment. Immediately upon doing so, however, he courted the opprobrium of the officers whose pay packets would be significantly lighter as a result, and whose goodwill in the circumstances had already been tried by the restrictions recently implemented on their receiving of presents and on private trading. By the end of the year and into 1766, Clive's new policies spurred active resistance by some officers, a development that came to be called the White Mutiny.

One of Clive's chief reforms was to reorganize the company's army by dividing it into three brigades, each commanded by a colonel. In two of his colonels Clive as commander in chief was fortunate; in the third—Sir Robert Fletcher—however, he was not so blessed. Fletcher commanded the First Brigade based at Monghyr in Bihar. Like so many of his colleagues, including Clive, Fletcher had started his company service as a writer in Madras before transferring to the army. Irritatingly superior and, in the parlance of the time, a "bounder," Fletcher nonetheless rose in stature helped along by the patronage of Laurence Sulivan, which was a clear mark against him in Clive's estimation. What's more, Fletcher had begun to stir up his officers at Monghyr in opposition to Clive's reforms in pay and allowances. "From others," Clive wrote to Robert Orme in February, "not from me, you will learn what struggles are making throughout this settlement for what the Gentlemen call independency; I call it licentiousness and a struggle whether the immense revenues of Bengal, Bahar and Orissa shall go into the pockets of individuals or the Company. You know enough of me," he concluded, "to know that I do not readily give up a point."[13]

Clive's vow was soon realized. The next month he departed upcountry again, this time to attend the annual celebration known as the *Punyah* held by Moghul officials to mark the beginning of the new tax year. Motijihil, north of Plassey, was the site of the celebration, and Clive entered fully into the festivities only to be stopped short in their midst on April 29 when he was informed by letter from Colonel Fletcher that unless a certain perquisite called the double *batta*—given to officers serving in the field—was restored then most of them at Monghyr would resign effective May 15. Fletcher's words were potentially catastrophic for the company's position in Bihar and beyond because without officers, thousands of already discontented troops were likely to mutiny. His words were also a personal affront to Clive's policies and position for it had been he who had issued the order in

January that the *batta*—a leftover gift from the time of Mir Jafar—be abolished.

Clive's response was immediate and his rage was unbridled at the insolence and insubordination of Fletcher. He decided to go straight to Monghyr to see whether his very presence there might quash the potential mass resignation, as well as give him the opportunity to deal directly with the execrable Fletcher. The journey took two weeks, however, a slog through the early monsoon not unlike the one that he had taken to reach Plassey nine years earlier. Arriving at Monghyr, as it happened on May 15, the day that the officers had warned their resignation would take effect, Clive found that they in fact had departed a day earlier, leaving behind a restive fort but no apparent mutineers. To make sure that indeed all was quiet, upon entering the parade square he demanded the soldiers' immediate subordination. Having duly received it, he then said, "Now I am satisfied you are British soldiers and not, as I was erroneously informed, assassins."[14] From that moment the putative White Mutiny lost its heat, and in the goodwill that then ensued Clive chose to reward the uniformly dutiful sepoys with extra pay.

The mutinous officers themselves were not, however, so fortunate. In the days that followed they were rounded up easily, sent down to Calcutta, and from there placed aboard ships bound for England, their company and military careers over. Some of the officers pleaded for clemency, which, in a few cases, was granted. A court-martial was quickly established at Patna, its main defendant to be Colonel Fletcher, who, Clive was sure and rightly so, had been the main instigator of the officers' threatened actions. By July Fletcher, who had absconded in May, was found, arrested, and tried. He was found guilty of mutiny and cashiered. His military career was over, but nothing could be done to prevent his return to England as a rich man with, like many of his lesser mutineers, an equally large enmity for Clive about which he was voluble.

After the protracted tensions of the spring and the judicial proceedings against the mutineers, Clive not surprisingly was emotionally wrung out. The old complaint of "rheumatysm" had returned and soon he had fallen victim also to a nervous collapse. This being India, the strength-sapping recurrence of malaria also brought him low.

Altogether by November Clive was prostrate, dosing himself with opium and unable to do much of anything except remain in bed. For a man as robust as Clive generally was, the scene played out at Government House in Calcutta had thus become close to ignominious. His letters home—"above all follow the instructions of your mother; let her excellent example be your guide," as he had advised Ned in January in a constant refrain—ceased.[15] He became isolated and eventually depressed, longing for an end to his trying Indian sojourn and a return to the relative comforts of England.

In what proved to be his final months in India, Clive transacted very little business. He settled on his successor as governor, a longtime company servant, the trustworthy and devoted Henry Verelst. In order to inoculate still further the position of governor from suspicions that it brought rewards now unavailable to ordinary company traders, Clive took an oath in October prohibiting the governor from engaging in trade. Nevertheless, the oath had something of a hollow ring to it as Clive had benefited greatly from his current stay in Bengal: he would send home some £160,000, even though he had been there only about seventeen months. In his defense, most of this money came from recouping delayed payments on his jagir, but the wealth had accrued regardless. It was for this reason that he had earlier explained to his father that "I have not benefited or added to my fortune one farthing, nor shall I."[16] In point of fact this might have been true, but the remittances home had continued all the same, from cash to diamonds and precious stones.[17]

Despite the tortuous end to his final term in Bengal, Clive throughout had lived exceedingly well. He had expended thousands of pounds on all manner of creature comforts. As is usually the case with people, since acquiring his wealth Clive had lived up to it and this meant purchasing the best clothes or "wearing apparel," fine wines, high quality joints and other foods, and various "table expences."[18] The dignity of the governorship, of course, required that a certain standard be maintained, but there's little doubt that Clive had acquired a large appetite for the very best of material goods. If the size of a man's stomach is a reliable guide to his wealth in Georgian England, then Clive as rendered on canvas comes down to our own time as being a very rich man indeed.

Expensive tastes notwithstanding, Clive could be generous, as we have seen earlier, especially concerning his family. But beyond the familial circle he could demonstrate generosity too, especially in his decision in April of 1766 to endow a pension fund for company soldiers who had served in Bengal. The fund was one of the first of its kind anywhere, the money for it coming from a legacy originally given to Clive by Mir Jafar as part of the Plassey settlement. As the "Military Fund," it would be formalized in an agreement between Clive and the company in 1770 and capture under its terms of reference pensioners, as well as those who had been invalided or superannuated and, at one-quarter the usual payable rate for life, their widows.[19]

By the end of 1766 Clive had recovered well enough from his various emotional and physical ailments and therefore was eager to leave India for home. He had done his best to continue making the case in London of the value of the hard-won territories in India, writing to Lord Rockingham, who had served recently as prime minister and was the creator of a powerful parliamentary bloc known as the Rockingham Whigs, so "that your Lordship may have some idea how much the Nation has at stake in . . . the provinces of Bengal, Bahar, & Orissa." Evidence for the claim was then given by listing in detail the company's receipts for 1766, which totaled (to that time) just under four million pounds.[20] To drive home the point he informed his old political chief, the Duke of Newcastle, of the company's situation and value to the country in much the same way.[21]

"I cannot do the Company much more service in Bengal," Clive wrote to Margaret on January 1, 1767, and therefore "I think it high time to think of England." This letter was the first she had received from him in a very long time. Ordinarily they corresponded frequently, in a warm—"My Lord"; "Your affectionate wife"—if somewhat stilted tone, even for the era in which they lived.[22] So his protracted silence this time was unusual. Indeed, he would write in April that he "had not put pen to paper for these five months past." Regardless of the loose chronology Clive indeed was keen to sail for home being now, in his estimation, "tolerably well" and having recovered "from a nervous attack which I thought I could not survive it being so much beyond what I suffered even in England." He credited "ophium" with having "saved me . . . which has had a most surprising effect upon my original nervous disorder."[23]

Exactly four weeks later on January 29 the *Britannia* weighed anchor at Calcutta, and with a relieved Clive happily on board, the ship sailed for its distant namesake. After three spells spent in India over the preceding twenty-three years, Clive would never again return to the subcontinent. Upon his departure the outgoing governor took with him a staggering array of "curiosities," the bulk of this collection of swords, knives, armor, and other items coming to reside eventually at Powis Castle, where they remain today housed in its Clive Museum.[24] Some five-and-a-half months later on July 14 Clive was "in the Channel" within a few hours' landing at Portsmouth, he wrote to Margaret. And with, one supposes, a mixture of great relief and keen anticipation, he added, "I propose dining with you tomorrow at Berkeley Square."[25]

# Lord Clive

LORD AND LADY CLIVE were reunited, as planned, at their Berkeley Square town house on July 15, 1767. Over two years had passed since Clive had gone to India. To his children, he was something of a stranger, although thirteen-year-old Ned had written to him dutifully from Eton College, where he was an Oppidan (a non-scholarship student), and, when out of term, from home. Naturally eager to please a father with such a large and growing public reputation—"I shall endeavour to render myself worthy of your love and affection by improving and cultivating my mind with whatever is useful," he wrote in November 1766—Ned would eventually spend five years in India himself, as Governor of Madras from 1798 until 1803.[1]

During the early days following his arrival in London, Clive pursued a round of formal visits. He had an audience of King George and Queen Charlotte and, of course, went to East India Company headquarters on Leadenhall Street. The company's internecine struggles of which Clive had been a keen participant before leaving for Bengal in 1765 showed little sign of abating however, and he was drawn quickly back into their orbit. Laurence Sulivan remained a powerful member of the Court of Directors, and his animus toward Clive remained strong too.

But Sulivan was not Clive's only enemy. His reputation as some-one whose rewards from India had been too great was not something that he could easily overcome. The directors, accordingly, were uncongenial in their response to their returned proconsul, a state of mind made clear by their earlier refusal to prosecute John Johnstone for what Clive assured them had been gross insubordination. In any event, Johnstone remained the least of their worries as the new prime minister (since the summer of 1766), William Pitt—or the Earl of Chatham, as he had been raised—was committed to enforcing much closer regulation over the activities of the company. Such an eventuality would not come to pass for several years yet, but the direction the government wished to take in this regard had been made plain. Clive himself did not support the plan. Indeed, between his disagreement with the government on this point, and his ongoing strife with officials at Leadenhall Street—"I need not inform you of the cool situation I am at present in, with the Court of Directors," he wrote to a friend—Clive's return from India this time was certainly not wreathed in glory.[2]

Exacerbating Clive's troubles as he renewed his life in England was the reappearance of ill-health. He turned forty-two years old in September 1767, so by no means was he an old man. But his health belied this fact. His physical woes were chronic, and in the style established some years earlier, he took refuge again in Bath for a good part of his first autumn back in England. Understating his bad health as "indifferent," Clive was not able to attend to much business during the time he reclined at Bath, or later when he removed to Walcot and then on to London.[3] The answer to his health woes, he decided, was to go abroad; so within six months of returning home the ailing Clive—"the bilious disorder is at last arrived to such a height that there seems no other remedy but that of going to the South without delay"—Clive had packed up again, and together with Margaret and a substantial retinue of friends and servants departed Berkeley Square for the European continent on January 19, 1768.[4]

Arriving at Calais a week later, the large Clive party began a rather hectic nine-month European sojourn. Traveling by coach and bringing along with them the necessities required by those of their social station, they undertook a trip that was a formidable exercise in planning and logistics. Clive alone brought two large trunks, two seat boxes, and two valises. Plate and silver were also required. In short, living abroad and covering anywhere from thirty to fifty miles per day by coach (twice they endured sixty-three-mile days, or "ten and a half posts"), it is hard to see how this method of travel might improve Clive's debilitating health. But apparently it did. Paris and the South of France, and later Brussels, proved a tonic, and by the time he set foot on English soil again, at Dover on September 8, his health was at least stable.[5]

That autumn of 1768 brought a general election that saw Clive return to Parliament for the constituency of Shrewsbury. Meanwhile, he continued to purchase properties, such as Okehampton in Devon, in an attempt to enlarge the group of MPs offering their support of him in the Commons. The strategy was only moderately successful, however, and in any event the political jockeying and hurly-burly of life at Westminster did not much interest him now. Of greater concern to Clive was the continuing powerful influence that his enemy Laurence Sulivan had within the company's Court of Directors. Clive's jagir had never ceased to be a point of acrimony, and even though its continuation had been reaffirmed by the directors in a close vote in the autumn of 1767 prior to Clive's going abroad, it was an issue that simply would not stop percolating. Clive made sure to thank personally those who had voted "for the extension of my Jaghire," but even though its substantial payments gave him ongoing financial security, battling for its continuation was both politically bruising and psychologically draining.[6]

As much as the jagir remained a lively issue for Clive, the backdrop to it was the ongoing debate over the company's governance practices. By 1769 Clive was forever beyond being a military man, his life bound up inextricably in the politics of the company's position in India and at Westminster. But martial events in India could still have, of course, an impact on the company as when in the autumn of 1768 and into the New Year, Haidar Ali, a charismatic soldier who had carried out a successful coup against the Nawab of Mysore, attacked successfully English positions throughout the old battlegrounds of the Carnatic. Madras itself held fast, but reports out of India that reached England in the spring of 1769 had a depressing effect on the company, causing its stock price to fall precipitously. The directors' reaction was little short of panic, as many of their fortunes had been lost, and once again earnest discussion about what to do in India prevailed. In this context Clive brought forward his old idea of creating an office of governor-general, but when it became apparent that if the idea were to be actualized it would mean Henry Vansittart in the position, Clive balked. His erstwhile friend remained in Sulivan's camp and was therefore unacceptable to him. In haste, and in place of the gubernatorial idea, it was suggested that a trio of supervisors go out to India, one of whom, inescapably, would be Vansittart, but would include also Luke Scrafton, a stalwart Clive supporter. The third, Francis Forde, as it turned out, was likewise strong for Clive and therefore a highly satisfactory choice to him. Off the three men duly sailed in September, but some three months later their ship sank without a trace after leaving Cape Town, and along with the doomed *Aurora* went too hopes for the success of the company triumvirate.

Into this gloomy atmosphere soon came another dose of bad news: famine had visited Bengal beginning in 1769. Severe drought was reported there and in parts of Orissa and Bihar by September of that year, exacerbating the effects of an earlier light harvest. By the New Year deaths from starvation were occurring, and by mid-1770 the death toll was on a catastrophic scale. Indeed, it is thought that some one-third of the Bengali population—about ten million people—succumbed to starvation and disease between the years of 1770 and 1773. The company's laissez-faire response was no better or no worse than what could be expected in an age when corporate and government intervention in the natural workings of economy, state, society, and "Providence" was essentially non-existent.[7] Nonetheless some contemporaries did hold the company at least partially responsible for the disaster, and in so doing the company's fortunes, along with its devastated revenue base, contracted even more.

Clive's reputation as the ultimate parvenu left him especially vulnerable to public attacks in this period, and as they mounted he found himself increasingly isolated. One of Clive's, and the company's, most vociferous critics was Horace Walpole, son of Sir Robert Walpole, the former prime minister usually regarded to have been the first such office-holder in British history. Horace was both a longtime MP and a man of letters, well known after the 1764 publication of *The Castle of Otranto*, generally viewed as the first example of a gothic novel. He took a keen dislike to the nouveau riche India set, with Clive as his particular target. By the early 1770s, as we shall see, Walpole, and others such as the playwright Samuel Foote, would be in the vanguard of those intent on ridiculing Clive and the other company "nabobs."

In the meantime, Clive continued to be victimized by poor health, some of his complaints being of real physical import and others being what a later age would call psychosomatic. Regardless of the nature of his ailments, the new decade of the 1770s would not be kind to the middle-aged hero of Plassey. The company's fortunes continued at low ebb, and with the death of the former prime minister, George Grenville, in 1770 and the consolidation of power in the government of Lord North, the company came under even closer scrutiny. For Clive, Grenville's death meant the loss of a (political) friend that went along with the gradual loss, though not death, of other friends, notably Robert Orme. Even Stringer Lawrence was no longer found in Clive's circle, although his loss of friendship was more from aging and an understandable lack of contact than from—as it was with Orme—mutual disaffection. To top off Clive's personal slough of despond, his father, Richard, died at Styche Hall in May 1771. Ever Clive's champion, he died saddened by the deterioration of his son's health and aggrieved at the relentless attacks that rained down on his administrative record and vast wealth.

North's government preponderantly comprised "Tories," then in their infancy as a party political body, and the youthful prime minister began to seek out Clive as a source of information and expertise on the company's history and what might be done in the near future to regulate more closely its affairs. Parliament, as it had since the time of Pitt's administration, continued to put pressure on the company to reform. Rather than submit to the whims of interventionist MPs, however, the Court of Directors, under Laurence Sulivan's chairmanship, decided to try to position itself in front of the expected parliamentary clamor by drafting its own reform bill and introducing it. Sulivan, also an MP, did so on March 30, 1772, a date that became a clear marker in inaugurating Clive's personal annus horribilis. Nevertheless, in a robust, almost military manner, Clive rose to speak to the bill, prepared now to fight back hard against the growing volume of opprobrium being heaped on his head from both inside and outside the company. Horace Walpole had recently derided him again, unjustly blaming Clive for the calamity of the Bengal famine by writing in his best yellow journalistic form: "The groans of India have mounted to heaven, where the *heaven-born* General Lord Clive will certainly be disavowed."[8] Altogether, Clive found himself under steady attack with many of the company's directors who were happy to let him be the scapegoat for the alleged avarice and inhumanity of its Indian operations. In response to these attacks and to Sulivan's introduction of the company-designed reform bill, Clive offered a two-hour speech that was both eloquent and pugnacious. Arcing back seven years to when he had gone out to Bengal for the last time, he argued that upon his arrival he chose the best path open to him, an "intricate" one that demanded clearheaded implementation of policy and the strength to overcome those who were abusing the company's commercial position for personal gain. He emphasized to a rapt House that in so doing he was "determined to do my duty to the public although I should incur the odium of the whole settlement. . . . It was that conduct," he added with a flourish, "which enables me now, when the day of judgement is come, to look to my judges in the face."[9]

Clive's performance was brilliant in the baroque, theatrical manner common to eighteenth-century parliamentary oratory. Read today, however, it sounds overwrought and therefore almost comical. But in the crisis-ridden days of 1772, Clive's words offered a trumpet-blast of vindication, not only for the man himself but also for the public reputation of the beleaguered company—even if many, such as the vindictive Sulivan and his cohorts—were happy to let the company suffer if it meant the destruction of Clive's record. Indeed, between Walpole's ongoing sneers and the staging of Samuel Foote's *The Nabob*, a play that was a thinly veiled mockery of Clive, the company badly required a champion. And, ironically to his persecutors, no one fit the bill better than the bloodied but unbowed man of arms, Lord Clive.

Despite Clive's impassioned defense of his and the company's conduct, especially between the years 1765 and 1767, the press's blood was up. Their attacks remained vociferous and calumny knew no bounds, although in this the press showed its contemporary use as merely acting as the paid mouthpiece for whoever was willing to foot the bill. Showing, as always, the British penchant for class-based snobbery, Clive was described as "an obscure urchin" made wealthy and powerful by "that deluded Company."[10] And on it went. So too did the debates in Parliament until finally it was decided that before the bill introduced by Sulivan would be voted on, a select committee should be struck in order to inquire into the company's affairs in India as far back as 1756. The committee's thirty-one-member composition would include Clive and was chaired by Maj. Gen. John Burgoyne, something of an officer-dandy and, later, a lightweight playwright. He was not an ideal choice as chairman, but since the idea to strike a select committee had been his, so too became the task of chairing its proposed deliberations. Burgoyne's partiality in favor of Clive's enemies was likely, however. In any event, the committee began its work immediately, a job that would stretch until the spring of 1773.

For the next year, Clive's life was bound up in the workings of the Select Committee. He had already been engaged in steady correspondence with the Court of Directors over "charges respecting the management of the Company's affairs in Bengal, wherein I am made a party," and this would only continue.[11] Indeed, the acrimony between them intensified with Clive demanding that the case against him be turned over to two arbitrators, "one of whom shall be appointed by you, the other by me."[12] This particular suggestion was rejected, but in the meantime there was much extraparliamentary business to attend to, mainly his expanding real estate portfolio, including the recently purchased Claremont, near Esher, Surrey, a magnificent baroque pile that Clive would immediately reconstruct, with landscaping by the celebrated architect Lancelot "Capability" Brown. But despite Claremont's renewed grandeur, which came at a cost of some £100,000, Clive would never live there.

As the Select Committee went about its business, Clive thus also continued to go about his. The growing collection of houses, six altogether, he had purchased shrewdly and furnished elaborately.[13] At Berkeley Square and Claremont, as noted especially, he spent money lavishly. The houses had to be decorated and furnished, and while Clive's appreciation of art was rudimentary, his taste in this regard improved after he had befriended Benjamin West, the transplanted American painter then just beginning to gain a reputation as the chief interpreter of Britain's great imperial scenes; later, one of these would be his famous rendition of Clive's receiving of the *diwani* in 1765. During this period in Clive's life, West—"I will attend your Lordship to see those pictures"—became something of an artistic adviser to him.[14]

Clive also was able to consolidate his social position by finally being installed knight of the Bath in June 1772. And then in the autumn, following the death of Lord Powis, and with the help of Lord North, Clive was appointed Lord-Lieutenant of both Shropshire and Montgomery. The lord-lieutenancy was a clear mark of royal favor, as the office-holder became the monarch's county representative. As such, Clive was now the first man in his home shire, and he was therefore above, at least to some degree, the ongoing partisan battle taking place among the Select Committee.

And the full-throated battle within the Select Committee carried on throughout the summer and autumn of 1772 and into 1773. Clive was called on early in the proceedings to give evidence, and he did so in the full knowledge that the tenor of the Select Committee would likely result in them finding fault with him and therefore blackening his reputation in order to make it seem that the company's good commercial intentions and practices had been perverted by avaricious men on the spot. From time to time, and however unintentionally, Clive's remarks in this regard gave the other committee members reason to think they might be right, as when he responded while under cross-examination about the receiving of presents after the victory at Plassey with an impassioned "By God, at this moment, do I stand astonished at my own moderation!" But on the whole Clive gave as good as he got, and the whole exercise climaxed a year later when on May 19, 1773, he spoke again strongly in his own defense. Earlier that month Burgoyne decided that the time finally had come to bring the Select Committee's work to an end and in so doing point the finger of blame for the company's ongoing woes—it had, in the preceding autumn, been required to suspend paying dividends to its shareholders and request a million-pound loan from the government—at Clive as the chief of nabobs.[15]

Two days later on May 21, Clive rose once again from his seat to defend himself. Burgoyne was tenacious in his desire to destroy Clive's reputation and was considering a motion declaring that the £234,000 acquired by Clive at the time of Plassey from the wealth of the deposed

Siraj-ud-Daulah had come to him illegally. "Leave me my honour," an exhausted Clive pleaded with the House in a final riposte, "take away my fortune." Dramatically, he then left the chamber, and in the debate that ensued a majority of MPs chose to side with him. In so doing they rejected Burgoyne's passionate denunciation of Clive having had enriched himself, as he termed it, "to the dishonour and detriment of the State."[16]

Following his final words, and before knowing the outcome of the debate, Clive returned home to Berkeley Square, there to endure a fitful night until early the next morning when his old company friend and colleague, John Strachey, arrived from nearby Westminster to inform him with great happiness that he had won the day. Indeed, Alexander Wedderburn, another friend who had defended Clive to great effect in the House, had offered the encomium of: "Robert, Lord Clive, did, at the same time, render great and meritorious services to this country." The House had carried the motion with noisy enthusiasm and near unanimity, and with it the most trying year of Clive's life came to an end.

Clive's trial by parliamentary fire may have been over, and Sulivan's campaign against him dashed, but the damage done to his reputation remained, especially since neither the press nor men of letters such as Horace Walpole would let the issue die. "This every way great criminal," as Walpole charged, had gotten away with one in his view, a sentiment reinforced by Samuel Foote's play *The Nabob*, which opened that November in Dublin before doing so in London in 1774.[17] In Foote's hands, the lead character, Sir Matthew Mite, is a shameless social climber and poser. In every respect he is made to fit the popular image of Clive as the nabob par excellence. It mattered little to either Foote or Walpole, it seems, that Clive had defended himself successfully against the charges and ultimately received the approbation of Parliament for his record in India. Instead, as Foote put it in his opening-act allusion to Clive, "Sir Matthew Mite, from the Indies, came thundering amongst us; and, profusely scattering the spoils of ruined provinces, corrupted virtue and alienated the affections of all the old friends to the family."[18] In the same vein, Walpole had moaned rhetorically in the summer of 1773, "What is England now? – A sink of Indian wealth, filled by nabobs and emptied by Maccaronis!"[19]

As much as the perpetuation of this retrograde popular image may have hurt Clive's pride, his parliamentary victory ended the necessity of the protracted debate over, and defense of, his life's work. Indeed, in the aftermath of the Select Committee's deliberations Clive found himself newly liberated. North's government, by now committed to reforming the company, did so with the Regulating Act of 1773, a piece of legislation that owed much to a long and detailed memorandum that Clive earlier had given to the prime minister. The absolved Clive participated fully in the parliamentary debates over its form and content, although unsurprisingly he did not agree with the result in every respect. But the act did make provision for a governor-general, the first holder of which, Warren Hastings, received Clive's strong recommendation. Indeed, Clive and Hastings had maintained their friendship throughout the previous year's tumult, which, opined Clive in a letter to Hastings when it was all over, had been the work of a "few envious and resentful individuals [who] turned the whole attack against me, and aimed at the ruin of my fortune and reputation, but the justice of the House of Commons defeated their intentions."[20] Moreover, in the interminable issue that was Clive's jagir, Hastings had never wavered in his support. As Clive put it in a letter to him in October, "I am much obliged by the care you have taken in remitting my Jaghire. The Directors have not complained of the amount drawn upon them, nor indeed did you give them the least foundation."[21]

By the end of 1773 Clive had thus regained his emotional footing and so becalmed had turned his attention more clearly to domestic pursuits. His burgeoning art collection was added to on a tour of Italy beginning in December. Arriving in Florence on January 2, 1774, he then moved on to Rome, where, among other appointments, he had an audience of Pope Clement XIV. Naples was to have been his eventual winter resting-place, but after a brief sojourn there hosted by Sir William Hamilton (who later would be famously cuckolded by Admiral Nelson), he decided to return to Rome, purchasing a few paintings while there and staying until March. By mid-May Clive was back in England, with a general election in view. When it eventually came, over three days in mid-October, he was able to expand further his band of parliamentary supporters to seven, including his son Ned, elected MP for Ludlow.[22]

In good health and high spirits, therefore, he removed to Shropshire for the summer, staying by turns at both Walcot and Oakly. The sunny summer was not to last, however. The autumn brought with it more rain than was usual, and in early November Clive took ill. As often happened with him, what started out as a small complaint—this time a cold—turned into something larger, and all the old problems connected with his "rheumatysm" appeared again. Once more Clive sought the healing waters of Bath, but when they did not satisfy, he moved on to London, arriving at Berkeley Square on November 20. The next two days were hellish, as Clive suffered from acute abdominal pain, which he sought to ameliorate with his long-trusted medicinal standby, opium. Doped up on the powerful narcotic and suffering from intense pain when its effects wore off, Clive became severely depressed and in a fit of absence of mind on the morning of November 22 did something drastic. Years earlier in Madras, Clive may have tried to commit suicide while in the throes of one of his early periods of depression.[23] This time, however, at home in London, he succeeded. Excusing himself from playing a table game with Margaret and a few others, he went to the water closet. When he did not return, his concerned wife sought him out, opened the door, and found him dead; his throat had been slit by his own hand with a penknife. Clive was just forty-nine years old.

In the days that followed, the scandal that would surely have followed if news of the form and manner of Clive's death had been made public was avoided by his quiet funeral, an event that took place a week later at the small parish church of St. Margaret of Antioch in his remote home village of Moreton Say. That he had died by his own hand meant that Clive's grave within the church was unmarked, and remains so to this day, although on the exterior of the church beside the porch a plaque was later affixed. It reads: "Robert Lord Clive KB 1725–1774, Founder of the British Empire in India, baptised and buried in this Church." His great wealth—approximately £500,000—was settled upon his wife and children, with Ned as the first-born son naturally benefitting especially. Later, in 1784, Ned would marry Lady Henrietta Antonia Herbert, daughter of the earl of Powis, a move that put the finishing touches on the Clives' rise in the world. Twenty years after that in 1804, Ned would be ennobled as the first earl of Powis (third creation). The journey to wealth and social prominence begun by Robert Clive in 1742 when he had been named an entry-level writer in the East India Company was now complete. So too by then was the founding of British India. The fact that Clive was thirty-years dead in an unmarked grave, it might be said, was almost beside the point.

# Notes

## Chapter 1

1. A. Mervyn Davies, *Clive of Plassey: A Biography* (New York: Charles Scribner's Sons, 1939), 19.
2. See Harold Perkin, *The Rise of Professional Society: England since 1880* (London: Routledge, 1989).
3. "Family Search Genealogical Records": Richard Clive (c. 1694–1771), http://histfam.familysearch.org.
4. H. C. G. Matthew and Brian Harrison, eds., *Oxford Dictionary of National Biography: In Association with the British Academy: From the Earliest Times to the Year 2000.* (Oxford: Oxford University Press, 2004), 12:166–77 (hereafter cited as *ODNB*).
5. Ibid.
6. Quoted in Abraham Eraly, *The Mughal Throne: The Saga of India's Great Emperors* (London: Weidenfeld & Nicolson, 2003), 279.
7. This sketch of the East India Company, and its initial interaction with the Mughal Empire, is based mainly on John Keay's *The Honourable Company: A History of The English East India Company* (London: HarperCollins, 1991), chaps. 1–4, and on Eraly, *The Mughal Throne*, chap. 7.
8. *ODNB* 12:166.

## Chapter 2

1. Richard Holmes, *Sahib: The British Soldier in India, 1750–1914* (London: HarperCollins, 2005), 499.
2. British Library, MSS Eur G37, 7/14/f. 1, Clive to Richard Clive, September 10, 1744 (hereafter cited as BL).
3. Ibid.
4. Ibid.
5. Keay, *Honourable Company*, 68.
6. BL, MSS Eur G37, 7/14/f. 1, Clive to Richard Clive, September 10, 1744.
7. Ibid.

8. National Library of Wales, CR12/1/f. 15, Clive to George Clive, February 16, 1745 (hereafter cited as NLW).

9. The company library is thought to have been established by Elihu Yale, president of Fort St. George from 1687 until 1692. Afflicted by a self-induced scandal, however, he was removed from the presidency by the Court of Directors over corruption charges. Later, in 1718, the Boston-born Yale would help to endow the college at New Haven, Connecticut, that would bear his name.

10. See Keay, *Honourable Company*, chap. 14.

11. Quoted in Mark Bence-Jones, *Clive of India* (London: Constable, 1974), 21.

12. Quoted in Sir George Forrest, *Life of Lord Clive* (London: Cassell, 1918), 1:61.

13. Thomas George Percival Spear, *Master of Bengal: Clive and his India* (London: Thames and Hudson, 1975), 44–45.

14. BL, Add MSS 44061, f. 7, Clive to Robert Orme, March 8, 1762.

15. Ibid.

16. Quoted in Richard Owen Cambridge, *Account of the War in India between the English and French on the coast of Coromandel, from the year 1750 to the year 1760* (Dublin: George and Alexander Ewing, 1761), 14.

### Chapter 3

1. Eraly, *Mughal Throne*, chap. 10.

2. Keay, *Honourable Company*, chap. 12.

3. Sir John Malcolm, *The Life of Robert, Lord Clive: Collected from family papers communicated by the Earl of Powis* (London: J. Murray, 1836), 1:39.

4. Quoted in BL, MS Eur. Orme, vol. 1, 219–25.

5. Quoted in Cambridge, *Account of the War*, 67.

6. NLW, CR12/1/f. 12, Clive to George Clive, June 30, 1749.

7. ODNB.

8. NLW, CR1/3/f. 5, Clive to Robert Brown, December 13, 1750.

9. Clive, "Considerations on the former and present state of the East India Company," November 24, 1772, BL, Home Miscellaneous Series, vol. 211.

10. NLW, CR1/5/f. 3, Robert Orme to Clive, August 29, 1751.

11. Robert Orme, *History of the Military Transactions of the British Nation in Indostan, from the year 1745* (London: John Nourse, 1763), 1:183.

12. C. Brad Faught, *Gordon: Victorian Hero* (Washington, DC: Potomac Books, 2008), 88.

13. Fort St. David, "Consultations," October 21, 1751, BL, Oriental and India Office Collection (hereafter cited as OIOC).

14. Orme, *History of the Military Transactions*, 1:192.

15. Ibid., 194.

16. Ibid., 195.

17. BL, MSS Eur G37, 7/14/f. 21, Rebecca Clive to Clive, December 16, 1752.

18. Fort St. David, "Consultations," December 9, 1751, BL, OIOC.

19. BL, Orme MSS, vol. 2, Lawrence to Clive, April 16, 1752.

20. Dan Cruickshank, *London's Sinful Secret: The Bawdy History and Very Public Passions of London's Georgian Age* (New York: St. Martin's, 2010), 81–82.

21. BL, Orme MSS, vol. 288, John Dalton to Clive, October 21, 1752.

22. Margaret MacMillan, *Women of the Raj: The Mothers, Wives, and Daughters of the British Empire in India* (Toronto: Penguin, 2005), 1–2.

23. Linda Colley, "The Mitchell election division, March 24, 1755," *Bulletin of the Institute of Historical Research* XLIX (1976): 80–107.

24. BL, Orme MSS, vol. 288, n.d.

### *Chapter 4*

1. Keay, *Honourable Company*, 131.

2. NLW, CR1/3/f. 16, Clive to Richard Clive, February 14, 1756.

3. BL, MSS Eur G37, 22/1/f. 24, Roger Drake to Clive, February 8, 1757.

4. See Michael Edwardes, *Plassey: The Founding of an Empire* (London: Hamish Hamilton, 1969), chap. 7.

5. Linda Colley, *Captives: Britain, Empire, and the World, 1600–1850* (New York: Anchor Books, 2004), 255.

6. NLW, CR1/1/f. 14, Clive to Roger Drake, October 7, 1756; and BL, MSS Eur G37/4/1/f. 1, Clive to Directors, October 11, 1756.

7. NLW, CR1/1f. 18, Clive to Roger Drake, October 7, 1756.

8. NLW, CR1/1/f. 11, Clive to William Mabbott, October 6, 1756.

9. Quoted in Samuel Charles Hill, *Bengal in 1756–1757, a selection of public and private papers dealing with the affairs of the British in Bengal during the reign of Siraj-Uddaula; with notes and an introduction* (London: Murray, 1905), 1:239.

10. Ibid., 227.

11. NLW, CR1/2/f. 3, Clive to George Pigot, January 8, 1757.

12. BL, MSS Eur G37/1/3/ f. 3.

13. NLW, CR1/2/f. 15, Clive to George Pigot and the Select Committee, January 28, 1757.

14. NLW, CR1/2/f. 7, Clive to George Pigot, January 8, 1757.

15. Quoted in Hill, *Bengal*, 2:96.

16. BL, MSS Eur G37/22/1/f. 13, James Killpatrick to Clive, January 11, 1757.

17. NLW, CR1/2/f. 10, Clive to Select Committee, January 20, 1757.

18. NLW, CR/1/2/f. 24, Clive to Select Committee, February 1, 1757.

19. Quoted in Hill, *Bengal*, 2:243.

20. NLW, CR1/2/f. 54, Clive to Peter Renault, March 9, 1757.

21. NLW, CR1/2/f. 60, Clive to Peter Renault, March 13, 1757.

22. BL, MSS Eur G37, 22/2/f. 2, Roger Drake to Clive et al., April 4, 1757.

23. Quoted in Hill, *Bengal*, 2:243.

24. See John Gallagher and Ronald Robinson, "The Imperialism of Free Trade," *The Economic History Review* 6, no. 1, second series (1953).

25. Quoted in Hill, *Bengal*, 2:383.

26. NLW, CR1/6/f. 1, Clive to Select Committee, June 15, 1757.

27. BL, MSS Eur G37, 5/16/ff. 1, 3, Eyre Coote to Clive, June 19, 1757.

28. Quoted in Hill, *Bengal*, 2:420; and NLW, CR1/6/f. 4, Clive to Select Committee, June 20, 1757.

29. NLW, CR1/6/f. 4, Clive to Select Committee, June 21, 1757.

30. NLW, CR1/6/f. 3, Clive to Select Committee, June 19, 1757.

31. BL, MSS Eur G37, 1/3/f. 11.

32. Quoted in Bence-Jones, *Clive of India*, 174.

33. See, for example, K. M. Pannikar, *Asia and Western Dominance: A Survey of the Vasco da Gama epoch of Asian history, 1498–1945* (London: G. Allen & Unwin, 1959), 79.

34. NLW, CR1/6/f. 5, Clive to Select Committee, June 23, 1757.

35. Clive thought the Nawab's army was closer in size to sixty thousand men. NLW, CR1/3/f. 69, Clive to Richard Clive, August 19, 1757.

36. Quoted in Orme, *History of the Military Transactions*, 2:174.

37. NLW, CR1/6/f. 5, Clive to Select Committee, June 24, 1757.

38. NLW, CR1/6/f. 5, Clive to the Select Committee, June 23, 1757.

39. NLW, CR1/6/f. 5, Clive to Select Committee, June 24, 1757.

40. NLW, CR1/6.f. 5, Clive to Select Committee, June 23, 1757.

41. BL, MSS Eur G37, 22/4/f. 43, Select Committee to Clive, June 29, 1757.

42. NLW, CR1/3/f. 65, Clive to William Belchier, August 21, 1757.

43. NLW, CR1/3/f. 69, Clive to Richard Clive, August 19, 1757.

44. NLW, CR1/6/f. 9, Clive to Select Committee, June 30, 1757.

45. NLW, CR1/6/f. 11, Clive to Select Committee, June 30, 1757.

46. NLW, CR1/6/f. 12, Clive to Select Committee, July 4, 1757.

47. NLW, CR1/6/f. 12, Clive to Select Committee, July 2, 1757.

48. NLW, CR1/3/f. 71, Clive to Richard Clive, August 19, 1757.

### Chapter 5

1. NLW, CR1/3/f. 91, Clive to Robert Orme, August 7, 1758.

2. NLW, CR1/3/f. 65, Clive to William Belchier, August 21, 1757.

3. NLW, CR1/3/f. 67, Clive to Lord Barrington, August 21, 1757.

4. NLW, CR1/3/ff. 91–92, Clive to Robert Orme, August 7, 1758.

5. Quoted in Hill, *Bengal*, 2:437.

6. BL, Home Miscellaneous Series, vol. 193, Clive to Mir Jafar, September 3, 1757.

7. NLW, CR1/3/f. 173, Clive to Stephen Law, December 29, 1758.

8. NLW, CR12/1/f.15, George Clive to Clive, March 12, 1758.

9. NLW, CR12/1/f. 30, Warren Hastings to Clive, January 30, 1760.

10. BL, Add MSS 29131, ff. 3, 19, 29, 55, Clive to Hastings, August 15, September 18, October 8, 1758, February 10, 1759.

11. *Parliamentary Debates*, House of Commons, December 12, 1757.

12. BL, MSS Eur G37/15/17/ff. 3–4, Clive to William Pitt, January 1, 1757.

13. See Edward Pearce, *Pitt the Elder: Man of War* (London: Pimlico, 2011), 312.

14. NLW, CE1/1.

15. BL, MSS Eur G37/1/5/f. 1, [Calcutta European Community] Letter to Clive, December 5, 1759.

16. BL, MSS Eur G37/15/5/f. 3, Clive to Laurence Sulivan, February 20, 1759.

17. Mir Jafar's son and natural successor, Miran, had died earlier that year in grisly but spectacular fashion after being struck in the head by lightning.

18. Their third son, Robert (Bob), born in 1759, was ill and had been left behind in a doctor's care in Calcutta. He died in 1760. Another baby boy, Richard, who had remained in England when the Clives returned to India in 1755, had died in October 1756. BL, MSS Eur G37/7/25/f. 1, A. Kelsall to Clive, October 12, 1756.

19. BL, MSS Eur G37/7/14/f. 25, Rebecca Clive to Margaret Clive, March 30, 1758.

20. NLW, R3/1/f. 2, Clive to George Clive, March 21, 1761.

21. BL, MSS Eur G37/7/14/f. 23, Rebecca Clive to Clive, December 26, 1758.

22. NLW, CR12/1/f. 19, Stringer Lawrence to Clive, October 11, 1758.

23. NLW, R3/1/f. 1, Clive to George Clive, October 4, 1760.

24. Quoted in Malcolm, *Life of Robert, Lord Clive*, 195.

25. NLW, R3/1/f. 4, Clive to George Clive, August 5, 1761.

26. BL, MSS Eur G37/1/19/ff. 11, 3, April 28, 1764.

27. BL, Add MSS 32970, f. 71, Clive to Richard Clive, September 25, 1765.

28. NLW, CE/1, "Indenture of Agreement" between Clive and the East India Company, May 16, 1764.

29. NLW, EW1/2, "Joyners Day Book 1765."

30. NLW, R3/1/f. 3, Clive to George Clive, May 6, 1761.

31. BL, MSS Eur G37/15/1/f. 1, Clive to Lady Clive, June 4, 1764.

32. BL, MSS Eur G37/15/1/f. 3, Clive to Lady Clive, October 11, 1764.

### Chapter 6

1. BL, MSS Eur G37/15/1/f. 3, Clive to Lady Clive, October 11, 1764.

2. BL, MSS Eur G37/3/4/f. 8, Clive to Lady Clive, January 31, 1766.

3. BL, MSS Eur G37/15/1/f. 9, Clive to Lady Clive, January 6, 1765.

4. BL, MSS Eur G37/15/3/f. 1, Clive to John Carnac, May 3, 1765.

5. NLW, R3/2/f. 12, Edward Clive to Clive, March 31, 1766.

6. NLW, CR1/1/f. 11, Clive to William Mabbott, October 6, 1756.

7. BL, MSS Eur G37/15/3/f. 1, Clive to John Carnac, May 3, 1765.

8. Quoted in Forrest, *Life of Lord Clive*, 2:258.

9. NLW, CR5/1/f. 1, Clive to East India Company Court of Directors, August 28, 1767.

10. BL, Add MSS 32970, f. 71, Clive to Richard Clive, September 25, 1765.

11. Ibid.

12. BL, MSS Eur G37/15/17/f. 4, Clive to William Pitt, January 1, 1759.

13. BL, Add MSS 44061, f. 11, Clive to Robert Orme, February 5, 1766.

14. NLW, CR2/4, personal testimony as to Clive's actions in 1766; anonymous.

15. BL, MSS Eur G37/3/4/f. 3, Clive to Edward Clive, January 31, 1766.

16. BL, Add MSS 32970, f. 71, Clive to Richard Clive, September 25, 1765.

17. BL, MSS Eur G37/15/1/f. 7, Clive to Lady Clive, January 7, 1765. Also, NLW, CF3.

18. NLW, CF3, Clive's journals detailing his "State of Affairs" in Bengal, May 4, 1765, to December 31, 1766.

19. NLW, P2/2.

20. BL, Add MSS 32977, ff. 27, 30, Clive to the Marquis of Rockingham, September 6, 1766.

21. BL, Add MSS 32982, f. 355, Newcastle Papers.

22. NLW, R3/2, ff. 22, 1765–1767.

23. BL, MSS Eur G37/3/4/ff. 19, 21, Clive to Lady Clive, January 1, 1767, April 24, 1767.

24. See Mildred Archer, Christopher Rowel, and Robert Skelton, *Treasures from India: The Clive Collection at Powis Castle* (New York: Meredith Press, 1987).

25. BL, MSS Eur G37/3/4/f. 23, Clive to Lady Clive, July 14, 1767.

#### Chapter 7

1. NLW, R3/2/f. 13, Edward Clive to Clive, November 9, 1766.

2. NLW, CR4/2/f. 1, Clive to Sir James Hodges, November 28, 1767.

3. NLW, CR5/1/f. 1, Clive to East India Company Court of Directors, August 28, 1767.

4. NLW, CR4/2/f. 57, Clive to John Cale, January 19, 1768.

5. NLW, H11/1.

6. NLW, CE3/1, October 3, 1767.

7. See H. V. Bowen, *Revenue and Reform: The Indian Problem in British Politics, 1757–1773* (Cambridge: Cambridge University Press, 2002).

8. Horace Walpole, *Oxford Edition*, vol. VIII, 153.

9. *Parliamentary Debates*, House of Commons, March 30, 1772.

10. *Public Advertiser* (London), April 11, 1772.

11. NLW, CR5/1/f. 87, Clive to East India Company Court of Directors, January 12, 1772.
12. NLW, CR5/1/f. 91, Clive East India Company Court of Directors, January 2, 1773.
13. NLW, CR4/2/f. 126, Clive to Duke of Beaufort, November 11, 1771.
14. BL, MSS Eur G37/7/13/f. 13, Benjamin West to Clive, February 19, 1772.
15. Keay, *Honourable Company*, 384.
16. BL, Egerton MSS, 247, 134.
17. Horace Walpole, *Last Journals*, vol. I, 231.
18. Samuel Foote, *The Nabob: A Comedy in Three Acts* (1773), 37.
19. Walpole, *Horace Walpole's Correspondence*, vol. 23, edited by W. S. Lewis (Oxford: Oxford University Press, 1945), 400.
20. BL, Add MSS 29131, ff. 102–3, Clive to Warren Hastings, October 25, 1773.
21. NLW, CR6/2/f. 64, Clive to Warren Hastings, October 14, 1773.
22. NLW, P1/2, "Montgomeryshire Poll Book."
23. Malcolm, *Life of Robert, Lord Clive*, 1:47.

# Bibliographical Note

As Clive is a much-studied figure in the history of British India and of British imperialism more generally, works on him abound. To study his life effectively, therefore, requires familiarity with the many biographies that have been written about him since a writer using the nom de plume of Charles Caraccioli wrote his four-volume *Life of Robert, Lord Clive*, published in 1776. Another contemporaneous work was that written by Clive's erstwhile friend, Robert Orme, whose *History of the Military Transactions of the British Nation in Indostan*, first published in 1763, helped to make Clive a popular military figure in the mind of the (admittedly small, in those days) British reading public. In the nineteenth century James Mill's *History of British India* (1817), in which he cast a jaundiced eye at Clive in stark contrast to Orme's laudatory view of the hero of Plassey, became the standard work for a time. Then came two important studies of him, the first by Sir John Malcolm, *The Life of Robert, Lord Clive*, a full-scale three-volume biography published in 1836, followed in 1840 by Thomas Babington Macaulay's "Essay on Clive" in the *Edinburgh Review*. Malcolm's work was full of praise, but more importantly for the future historiography of his subject, it was based on Clive's private papers. Macaulay's essay took over where Malcolm's biography had left off, in that he synthesized Clive's record and achievement and, properly, gave both a sense of historical balance.

For the remainder of the Victorian era Malcolm and Macaulay held sway in shaping the way in which Clive was viewed, although increasingly the more morally censorious Victorians took a dislike to Clive because of his apparent venality. By the twentieth century the time had come for a new comprehensive biography, and it came from the pen of Sir George Forrest, whose *Life of Lord Clive*, published in 1918, was a two-volume successor to the work of Malcolm. Even almost a century later Forrest's work continues to stand up as a full-orbed treatment of Clive based on the author's meticulous use of the archival sources.

The Clive archives today are located principally in two places. The British Library in London is the repository of his papers that were kept originally at the old India Office Library. At some ninety-five boxes, they are a rich source, especially of Clive's official correspondence with the East India Company. The second indispensable cache of Clive's private papers is housed at the National Library of Wales in Aberystwyth. Contained in some thirty-five boxes they offer a wide assortment of letters and documents that were stored originally at Powis Castle before their gradual transferral to Aberystwyth, a process completed in the 1990s. No proper study of Clive can be undertaken without working in these two superbly kept archival collections.

Accordingly, recent biographies of Clive, as well as studies of the British in India in the eighteenth century more broadly, rely heavily on the materials housed in London and Aberystwyth. The best and most authoritative biography to emerge in the last couple of generations is that by Mark Bence-Jones. His *Clive of India*, published in 1974, set the standard for modern studies of the man, offering a rigorously balanced view of his record and character based on a comprehensive use of the archival sources and mastery of the secondary works. Strong too are Percival Spear's *Master of Bengal: Clive and his India*, published in 1975, and *Clive: the Heaven-Born General*, by Michael Edwardes (1977). Most recent of all is Robert Harvey's *Clive: The Life and Death of a British Emperor*. Published in 1998, it makes good use of the archival sources and the author is well acquainted with the Clive historiography. Harvey's interpretation leans toward the heroic but remains a long way from the hagiographic, which, in any case, in today's post-colonial world is a stance almost impossible to maintain.

# Index

# *About the Author*

C. Brad Faught is professor and chair of the Department of History at Tyndale University College in Toronto, where he teaches British and European history. A graduate of the Universities of Oxford and Toronto, he is a fellow of the Royal Historical Society and a senior fellow of Massey College at the University of Toronto. He is author of *The Oxford Movement: A Thematic History of the Tractarians and Their Times* (2003); *Gordon: Victorian Hero* (2008); *The New A-Z of Empire: A Concise Handbook of British Imperial History* (2011); and *Into Africa: The Imperial Life of Margery Perham* (2012).